follow your instincts

follow your instincts

A self-discovery journey
for personal empowerment

Lillian Monterrey

Monterrey Publishing, Inc.

Follow Your Instincts
A Self-discovery Journey for Personal Empowerment
by Lillian Monterrey

Copyright © 2002 by Lillian Monterrey

Cover Design: Wendi Gelfound
Editorial: Ivette Gonzalez

All rights reserved. No part of this book may be reproduced or transmitted in any form or by any means, electronic or mechanical, including photocopying, recording or by any information storage and retrieval system, or otherwise be copied for public or private use - without written permission from the author/publisher.

Library of Congress Control Number: 2002090492
ISBN: 0-9717189-0-3

Published and distributed in the United States by:

Monterrey Publishing, Inc.
15476 N. W. 77 Court # 706
Miami Lakes, Florida 33016
For orders: www.followyourinstincts.net

Printed in the United States of America

This Book is Dedicated to:

You

*For your courage to grow and be
Your True Self.*

this a gift from your proud daughter

Follow your instincts.

May you continue on your new life

Best Wishes,

Love,

Lillian Monterey

Trust the instinct to the end, though you can render no reason.

- Ralph Waldo Emerson

Follow Your Instincts

TABLE OF CONTENTS

Chapter 1. What Are Instincts and How Can They Benefit Your Life *7*

Chapter 2. Social Instinct -- Relationship with Yourself and Relationships with Others. *19*

Chapter 3. Security Instinct -- Self-preservation and Communication. *67*

Chapter 4. Sex Instinct -- Sexual Identity and Sexual Relations. *111*

Chapter 5. Be Assertive and Follow Your Instincts *145*

Chapter 6. Learn About Anger and Eliminate Resentments *159*

Chapter 7. Manage Your Fears and Eliminate Unnecessary Ones *183*

Chapter 8. Free Yourself from Guilt – Know When Guilt is Being Used to Manipulate You *205*

Chapter 9. Connect with Your Instincts – Connect with Wealth *223*

Chapter 10. Follow Your Instincts to Achieve Success, Wealth and Happiness *249*

Acknowledgments

I would like to thank with love and gratitude all the wonderful people who helped make this book possible:

In particular to all the attendees of my seminars, who taught me so much and encouraged me to put my ideas down on paper. To my friend, Dr. Robert Hersh, who inspired, motivated, and helped me believe I needed to write this book.

To all my friends who helped in the different stages of this book: Christopher Sheehan, Maria Christina Abal, Luisette Motta, Margaret Lyles, Jessie Fernandez, Hilda Hevia, Susanna Tarjan, Catherine Esposito, Gary Davis, Janet and John Gardiner, and my wonderful neighbors, Juan and Josefina Benitez. Special thanks to my friends, Wendi Gelfound, for her dedication and long hours in the wonderful art designing of the book cover, and Ivette Gonzalez, for her remarkable editing that included many long nights and week-ends.

Last, but not least, my family for their love and support, especially my nieces, Annie Monterrey and Adriana Oliva, my sister-in-law, Dini Monterrey, and most importantly, my husband, Bob Acosta, for his unconditional support and encouragement.

INTRODUCTION

Instincts influence everything you do. Everything that happens in your life has to do with instincts in one way or another. Instincts address your basic needs. When you connect with your instincts, you are able to control your life; your life does not control you!

This book is about God's greatest gift - your instincts!

You were born programmed perfectly with the instinct blueprint. This book is about helping you understand, connect with, and follow that blueprint. In addition to assisting in your survival, your instincts' purpose is also to guide you in creating happiness, success, and wealth.

Some authors write about self-esteem, others write about relationships, others write about how to become successful and make money, others write about communication skills, and others write about sex, sexuality or sexual identity. However, rarely have they told you all of these things are part of your instincts.

What I am writing about is a way for you to get in touch with the excellence inside you. The objective of this book is to give you information that will bring new meaning to your life. I hope you use this information by first applying it to yourself. Then, pass it on to help family members, friends, neighbors, coworkers, and eventually, take this knowledge everywhere you go.

I trust the information in this book will be as enlightening to you as it has been to me. I dedicate this book to the most important person in the world - YOU.

To get the most out of this book:

1. Read and re-read this book.
2. Use this book as a reference manual for a successful and happy life.

   GOOD LUCK!!!

PREFACE

I grew up in a middle-class Spanish family in Havana, Cuba, where my mother was a famous actress and my father was a prominent businessman. Because both parents had busy careers, my grandmother practically raised me.

As a child, I was a chubby little girl. I had made food my best friend. I remember the mean things the other children said about me. My parents took me to all kinds of different doctors to help me lose weight to no avail. They even forced me to take ballet lessons, which I hated, to see if that would help me lose weight.

When I was fourteen years old, in 1970, we came to the United States, leaving behind family, friends, and all of our possessions. It was a very difficult cultural change, considering that I did not speak English. At this time, my eating disorder, in the form of anorexia, bulimia, and compulsive overeating, took off. I was so unhappy with my life that at one time I almost died of anorexia by not eating for one month. Another time, I almost died of bulimia when I took 28 laxatives. The third time, I was so disgusted with my life, as a result of not feeling loved, that I tried to end it. Consequently, I faced death three times as a result of being unhappy.

My life was a mess physically, emotionally, and spiritually. What I wanted most was to be able to have a healthy relationship with a man and to feel loved. It was not until I was 26 years old, when I discovered a 12-step program to deal with my eating disorder, that my life began to change.

It took four years in a 12-step program for me to get slightly better. Then, I discovered a self-inventory process that helped me understand what was really happening to me. This process helped me understand my feelings and emotions and, more importantly, how I could manage them. The most valuable gift the personal inventory process gave me was reconnecting with my instincts and my true Self.

Fascinated by the information I had discovered, I began to teach this self-inventory process in English as well as in Spanish. This process teaches you the reasons why you have resentments and how to eliminate them. You learn to understand your fears and eliminate those fears you do not desire, as well as how to use fear as a barometer to know that something is wrong (not all fears are bad). You also learn to eliminate guilt and to not allow anyone to manipulate you with it, and more importantly, how instincts are part of your existence.

People from various South American countries were exposed to these workshops, and I began to travel internationally with this information. Through the experience of teaching the inventory process, I became more aware of the importance of people understanding their instincts, and I then developed seminars to specifically teach about instincts.

This book's primary objective is to get you in touch with your instincts and recognize the effects they have in your life.

I pray this book reaches you early in your life to help you avoid unnecessary years of pain. This information truly changed my life and this is the reason I made the decision to write about instincts. I have written this book for you from my heart with love. I hope this information helps change your life, as it did mine, to one of happiness.

Happiness is an inside job!

There is only one success – to be able to spend your life in your own way.

- Christopher Morley

Chapter 1

WHAT ARE INSTINCTS AND HOW CAN THEY BENEFIT YOUR LIFE

Have you ever thought one thing, felt something else, and ended up saying something completely different?

Your instinct connection was perfect when you were born. What happened to some of us was that as children the adults in our lives ("the Big people" -- as I call them) began to influence our thinking by creating programs that were in conflict with our instincts.

When you were hurt as a child and went to an adult (perhaps your mother or father) to express your hurt feelings, they might have said something like: "That was not so bad...You are not supposed to feel that way." This created confusion between your God-given instincts and what "the big people" in your life were telling you. Therefore, you learned at a very young age not to express or honor your feelings. You created the scenario of feeling one thing while thinking something else, and yet expressing something totally different. What you needed then was assistance in directing you to the instinct blueprint.

You will be teaching yourself to reconnect with the information the Creator placed inside you, and it will help you discover yourself through your instincts. What you will achieve is self-understanding.

Self - understanding is knowing yourself. It allows you to discover the kind of person you are, and the person you would like to become. It allows you to be free to become the best person God intended you to be.

Instincts are part of your subconscious mind placed there by the Creator, and intellect is part of the conscious mind. The conflict appears when the conscious mind has different information than the subconscious. Your conscious mind has been programmed by "the big people" in your life (mother, father, grandparents, teachers, ministers, etc.).

THIS BOOK WILL ASSIST YOU TO RE-CONNECT WITH YOUR INSTINCTS, SO THAT YOU CAN EXPRESS EXACTLY WHAT YOU THINK AND FEEL.

Instinct – an impulse directing you to behave in a certain direction.

Instincts are within our entire being. Our body functions like a computer system. It has programs for every function. For instance, there is a program for our breathing. We do not have to force ourselves to breathe; we do it automatically, even when we sleep. We also have a blood circulation program that keeps our blood circulating all the time. However, I am only going to concentrate on the program called - *instincts*. There is no knowledge behind instincts. An instinct is a behavior pattern that does not need to be learned.

An instinct is a built-in behavior pattern that is in humans as well as animals as a method of survival.

According to Webster's dictionary (my source of reference throughout this book), an instinct is:

1. An inborn pattern of activity or tendency to action common to a given biological species.
2. A natural impulse, inclination or aptitude.
3. A natural intuitive power.
4. An impulse.
5. An urge animated by some inner force.
6. A precise inherited form of behavior.

Instincts are a driving force, which cause action in a particular behavioral pattern. As a result of evolution, we have been left with instinctual predisposition to act and react for our survival.

We have Three Basic Instincts:

1. Social (RELATIONSHIPS), which includes the relationship with yourself and relationships with others.

2. Security (SELF-PRESERVATION), which includes food, shelter, money as a medium of exchange, personal space (boundaries), time, talent, information, opportunity, and most importantly, communication.

3. Sexual (PROCREATION), which includes sexual identity and sexual relations.

Throughout this book you will notice that there are many cross-references between chapters. You may think you are reading things twice. It is not your imagination. It is because the subject matter interconnects and overlaps. As you progress in your reading, you will become more aware of this interconnection, and the subject matter will become clearer to you.

The security instinct helped man to harvest food and construct shelter to ensure survival. The sexual instinct led man to reproduce so that we could populate the earth. In turn, the social instinct had man care for one another and live in society to ensure their survival.

Without instincts we would not be able to function as human beings!

The instinct program God placed inside us is geared toward helping us cope in every area of our lives. This can be clearly observed in all of the animal kingdom Understanding our instincts is very important because through connection with them, we get to know ourselves. As an additional benefit, we will get to know our fellow man. All humans have the same instincts.

God gave the animal kingdom (of which humans are a part) instincts to help them function on earth. The difference between animals and humans is the degree of intellect. *If you really want to get in touch with your instincts, it is necessary to understand the separation between intellect and instinct.*

Animals tend to depend more on instinct, whereas humans have, over the ages, reversed this and rely mostly on intellect. This is most unfortunate because instincts can be of great assistance to us in our lives.

The Newly Hatched Flea

An instinct is an inborn precise form of behavior. A good example of instincts can be seen in a new generation flea A flea egg hatches and the newly hatched flea, that has not seen or will ever see its parents, instinctively knows how to obtain food for survival. The flea has inherited a behavioral pattern that we call instinct. It is a gift from the Creator to the flea for its survival.

The Turtle

Another example can be seen in the turtle. When a turtle is hatched, it knows instinctively to go immediately to the water. His survival depends on getting there as quickly as possible. The turtle knows it must avoid being eaten by the ever-present predators.

Intuition --- Part of Your Instincts

Intuition is a personal spiritual experience. God talks to us through intuition. Intuition transcends reason. Sometimes our intellect could be telling us to behave in a particular way while our intuition is telling us to do something different. It is best to follow our intuition because intuition is the way God communicates with us.

Follow Your Instincts

Instinct is a direct communication from God to you. Intuition is a more indirect communication. *Not following your intuition will result in internal conflict. Always follow your intuition.*

Intuition is the Universe telling you how to behave in accordance with the Universal rules so that you can flow with the river of life.

Just as we are subject to the law of gravity, and could be in serious trouble if we ignore it, likewise we will be in serious trouble if we ignore *our instincts* and *intuition.* To not make use of these gifts is like driving a car with your eyes shut.

Pay attention to that voice inside you when it is trying to tell you something, even if what the voice is saying is different from your opinion. As you progress in connecting with your instincts you will become more aware of the validity of this phenomenon. Sometimes the Universe sends messages we do not want to hear, so we justify not listening by saying to ourselves the messages might be wrong. This is your intellect talking. When your intellect has information that is different from your instincts you become fragmented. Because the Universe is usually right, we should give intuitive messages more attention.

When we have a problem in life, we first process it with our instincts, and then with intellect. In doing so, most of the time we can find the answers to whatever may be happening. The idea is to connect instincts with intellect. If we still have questions, we can consult our concept of God. Usually the answer comes back to us in the form of intuition, or just a plain connection between instincts and intellect.

What Are Instincts and How Can They Benefit Your Life

Following Your Intuition Daily to Save Time

I have a cleaning lady that first cleans my home, and then my office. I have a back room in my office that is normally locked, but I leave it open on the day she cleans. One week I left the office in a rush and forgot to leave the back office open, and therefore I wanted to go home to give her the keys before she left my home to go to the office. On the way to the house I also needed to stop at the bank to make a deposit, but I was afraid the cleaning lady would leave my house, go to the office, and that I would miss her. I had the option of stopping at the bank, taking a chance I would have enough time before she left. The alternative was to go directly home in order not to miss her.

Not knowing how much longer the cleaning lady would be at my home, and not being able to talk to her because she does not answer the phone in my absence, I paused and asked God a simple question, "Should I stop at the bank to save time, or should I go directly home?" This question might seem ridiculous to you, but it saved me a lot of time.

The answer was to go straight to the bank. However, my intellect was telling me to go home first not to miss the cleaning lady. I decided to follow the Universe's answer and saved a lot of time. The interesting part was that when I arrived home the cleaning lady still had an hour of cleaning left to do.

YOUR CONNECTION WITH YOUR INTUITION IS DEVELOPED MORE EVERY TIME YOU ASK THE UNIVERSE FOR ANSWERS AND FOLLOW ITS SUGGESTIONS.

Follow Your Instincts

Following Your Intuition --- Another Example

I came home every day at lunchtime to exercise, have lunch, and work one hour or so on this book. I wanted no interruptions while I was writing; therefore, I did not answer my home phone. If I was needed, my husband, or the office, could call me on the cellular.

One day I was working on the book and the phone rang. I felt this intense need to answer. I asked the Universe if I should answer the telephone. The message was very clear to do so. It was a lady calling me from South America wanting some information about Overeaters Anonymous (a support group for eating disorders). If I had not answered, it would have meant this lady would have had to call back long distance for this information. Or worse, she may never have called back, and never received the information she needed.

Answers Lie Within

One morning I woke up to find my eyes very puffy with wrinkles. I did not know what was wrong with them. They had been tearing for a few days. I visited an eye doctor, who gave me a cream I needed to use twice a day for two weeks, and I was to follow up with him.

In the two-week period I saw no change in my eyes' condition, but went back to that doctor anyway. He said my eyes were okay, but I needed to place hot compresses on my eyelids while in the shower, and the puffiness would disappear. I asked him what was wrong with my eyes, and he said the tear gland was inflamed.

After following the eye doctor's recommendation for two more weeks and seeing no change, I decided to see a dermatologist, to define if there was something wrong with the eyelids.

The dermatologist said it was a condition caused by many years of sun exposure. To this statement, I immediately said silently to myself, "Cancel, cancel, doctor you are wrong." He then proceeded to prescribe a cream for me to apply to my eyelids twice a day. I went ahead and followed his directions. I had a reaction to this cream and my eyes got worse and puffier. I went back to this doctor and he prescribed yet another cream.

During this period, I developed a kidney infection and went to see my family practice doctor to whom I also showed my eyes, and he said the puffiness was from the kidney infection. The idea it could be from the kidneys made more sense to me. However, I had been seeing a homeopathic doctor for my menopausal symptoms, and I also decided also to check with him about my kidneys and puffiness in the eyes.

The homeopathic doctor prescribed a tea for me to drink 12 cups a day to clean my kidneys. He also said the puffiness of the eyes was from the kidneys. By this time two months had lapsed and my eyes were not better and I was very sad that I would be wrinkled before my time. I decided to ask God what could be wrong with my eyes and what had happened?

The answer came immediately! "You used a product that hurt your eyes." I went and checked the product I had used prior to this problem, and found the directions indicated not to apply it to the eyelids. I felt awful for not having read the instructions properly. The cream was made with vitamins A and C to improve and prevent wrinkles. I thought, because the product was only made with vitamins, it could not harm me.

I called the manufacturer of the product, and they explained Vitamin C was very harmful to the sensitive area of the eyelids.

I meditated and asked the Universe how to heal myself, since all of the doctors had failed. The answer was very simple: "Use an eye drop with some antihistamine since it is an allergic reaction to the product." I began to use the eye drops and some aloe vera on the eyelids. My eyes began to get better immediately and today they are back to normal.

The reason for my story is to show you that if I would have asked God first, and had followed my intuition from the beginning, I would have saved time, money and aggravation. Sometimes it's easy to forget something as simple as asking God for the answers.

ALWAYS CHECK WITH THE GOD INSIDE YOU BEFORE ACCEPTING ANY DIAGNOSIS.

SUMMARY

An instinct is an impulse directing you to behave in a certain direction.

By re-connecting yourself with your instincts you will be able to think, feel and communicate the same message. You will also be able to discover the real you.

Self-understanding is knowledge about yourself. It allows you to discover the kind of person you are and the person you would like to become. It allows you to be free to become the best person God intended you to be.

The Creator gave you instincts as a gift for you to live in a successful, abundant, and happy manner.

We have Three Basic Instincts:

1. Social (RELATIONSHIPS), which includes the relationship with yourself and relationships with others.
2. Security (SELF-PRESERVATION), which includes food, shelter, money as a medium of exchange, personal space boundaries), time, talent, information, opportunity, and most importantly, communication.
3. Sexual (PROCREATION), which includes sexual identity and sexual relations.

Intuition is the Universe telling you how to behave in accordance with the Universal rules so that you can flow with the river of life. Not following your intuition will result in internal conflict. *Always follow your intuition.*

The Creator is constantly helping you through intuition in your quest for success and happiness.

Open yourself to that gift!

The only way to have a friend is to be one.

-Ralph Waldo Emerson

Chapter 2

SOCIAL INSTINCT – RELATIONSHIP WITH YOURSELF AND RELATIONSHIPS WITH OTHERS

What is Social Instinct?

Social instinct is composed of two parts: relationship with yourself and relationships with others.

This chapter will help you connect with your social instinct. It will help you develop a better relationship with yourself by helping you connect with your self-esteem and your self-worth. It will assist you in developing better relationships with others.

1. Relationship with Yourself

You have to have, or you have to develop, a relationship with yourself. You have to become your own best friend by spending time with yourself, trusting yourself, honoring your decisions, keeping your word, accepting yourself with the good and the bad, and most importantly, loving yourself unconditionally.

The relationship you have with yourself is connected to your self-esteem. It includes:

>a. SELF-RESPECT - Self-respect is expressed by how you value yourself, how you think of yourself, your own sense of dignity, and most importantly, how you love yourself.

>b. PRIDE - Pride is a sense of feeling good about yourself. It is feeling good about your work and what you do, feeling good about your achievements and accomplishments.

Self-esteem

When you were born, you were connected with your instincts. As a child, if "the big people" (parents, grandparents, teachers, spiritual leaders) gave you messages different from what you felt inside, you began to disconnect from your instincts.

>Messages Like:

>>You are a dummy.
>>You will never amount to anything.
>>You need to be more like so and so.
>>You will never learn.
>>Your grades are too low.
>>You are stupid.
>>You can never do anything right.
>>You are too fat (or too slim).
>>You always do that.

Social Instinct – Relationship with Yourself and Relationship with Others

If you heard these messages as a child, you probably were robbed of your self-confidence and your self-esteem.

There are different levels of self-esteem, high and low. We can describe self-esteem on a scale of 1 to 10, one (1) being the lowest self-esteem and ten (10) the highest. Your job is to figure out where yours is.

HIGH SELF-ESTEEM
10
9
8
7 *Where are you*
6 *in this scale?*
5
4
3
2
1
LOW SELF-ESTEEM

You need to find out your level of self-esteem.

When you have high self-esteem you attract people and events to your life that will bring more success than you ever dreamed possible. You can deal with life on life's terms and produce changes in your life that will seem like miracles.

Even if you think you have high self-esteem, you can improve it, or at least become aware of what actions could possibly affect it in a negative manner.

Follow Your Instincts

Low Self-esteem Manifestation

If you have low self-esteem you will tend to:

1. Feel different than the rest of the world.
2. Tell yourself you cannot do anything right.
3. Be afraid of making mistakes, so you do not take risks.
4. Have difficulties making decisions.
5. Be a perfectionist.
6. Constantly "should" yourself (I should do this. – I should do that.).
7. Blame yourself for everything.
8. Think you are not good enough.
9. Feel a lot of guilt, especially about spending money on yourself, because you do not feel worthy of having nice things.
10. Constantly put yourself down for the way you look, think, feel, and act.
11. Get angry and defensive easily.
12. Constantly criticize yourself and take things personally.
13. Get depressed easily.
14. Not accept compliments or praise easily.
15. Deny trouble ---- pretend it does not exist.
16. Feel like a victim.
17. Look for outside things to feel worthy – better cars, houses, etc.
18. Believe good things will not happen to you.
19. Not feel lovable.
20. Normally be shy.
21. Procrastinate.
22. Not participate in life by isolating yourself.

If you can identify with some of these low self-esteem manifestations, this could be an indication you need to work on improving your self-esteem.

Your self-esteem manifests itself in every area of your life, such as your relationship with yourself, your relationship with others, and your relationship with your work and social activities. In other words, the lack of good self-esteem will become a problem.

People with high self-esteem are happy people who love their lives. They capitalize on their strengths to produce the results they want. They are also capable of accepting their weaknesses.

THIS BOOK IS ABOUT CREATING MIRACLES BY IMPROVING YOUR SELF-ESTEEM AND RECONNECTING YOU WITH YOUR GOD-GIVEN INSTINCTS.

What Really is Self-Esteem?

Self-esteem is the way you feel about yourself. It includes being able to respect and love yourself. It is a sense of pride about who you are. High self-esteem could be described as your ability to feel *lovable* and *capable*.

Your self-image determines how you behave. Every thought you process is connected with self-esteem, and it determines how much you accomplish in life and how happy you will be.

To improve your self-esteem you have to journey through the process of changing your thinking by changing what you say to yourself. Try to spend a day listening to everything you say and become aware of thoughts you have about yourself. This will help you discover negative patterns you need to change in order to improve your self-esteem.

The best way to discover how you see yourself is by analyzing how you treat yourself. The way you treat yourself is the way you see yourself. At this very moment ask, "How do I see myself?" A poor self-image will tell you, "I do not deserve _____."

Know you deserve the very best. God wants the best for you.

SELF-ESTEEM IS FEELING LOVABLE AND CAPABLE. IT IS AN ESSENTIAL PART OF YOUR RELATIONSHIP WITH YOURSELF.

What is the difference between self-esteem and self-worth?

Most people confuse self-worth with self-esteem.

SELF-ESTEEM --- is how you *feel* about who you are.

SELF-WORTH --- is the way you *think* about yourself.

To enhance your worthiness you have to become more and get more. To improve your self-esteem you have to enjoy what you have and who you are.
Love yourself unconditionally by accepting yourself just the way you are today with the understanding that you can improve. You might have areas in your life that need change and that's okay. We all have areas in our lives that

Social Instinct – Relationship with Yourself and Relationship with Others

we can improve, but the magic of good self-esteem lies in the ability to love oneself in spite of changes we might have to make.

Here are some suggestions to build a positive self-image:

1. Speak and think well of yourself.
2. Surround yourself with positive people.
3. Let people know how you expect to be treated.
4. Praise yourself and others.
5. Give and accept compliments.
6. Treat your body with love.
7. Develop the habit of experiencing pleasure without guilt.
8. Make it a point to be happy. Abraham Lincoln said, "Most people are as happy as they make up their minds to be."

The "I Love You" Story

When I was first exposed to the twelve-step program (a support group to empower change in people suffering from compulsive behavior disorders by addressing the physical, emotional, and spiritual aspects of life), I truly did not love myself. I remember one day, I was speaking with one of my sponsors on the telephone and he said, "Lillian, I want you to do me a favor. Go right now to the bathroom mirror and with the lipstick you use every day write I LOVE YOU, and when you're done come back to the telephone."

I felt what he was asking me to do was very stupid, but I wanted to improve my life. I was willing to do whatever was asked of me. With no questions asked, I went ahead and did it with tremendous difficulty because of my low self-esteem. When I came back to the telephone and told him it was done, he replied, "Now, I do not want you to erase it until I tell you to, so that every morning and evening you get to see that message from you to you."

After six months passed, I asked my mentor and friend, "How much longer should I have the I LOVE YOU in my bathroom mirror?"

"I am sorry, I forgot," he answered. "I only meant for you to have it on your mirror for a few weeks."

It is my belief God intended all along for me to have it on the mirror for six months. God was giving me the message to love myself and at the same time was helping me to improve my self-esteem.

If you feel you do not love yourself, or if you feel you could love yourself more, my message to you is (whether you are a male or a female) write on the mirror you see yourself in every day, I LOVE YOU!, and leave it there until you feel you do love yourself and your self-esteem has improved.

Say to yourself every morning and every evening: ILOVE YOU."

Good self-esteem will manifest itself in accordance with the degree you love yourself. *Begin to love yourself unconditionally!*

"Walk Tall and be Proud"

During the same period of time I had the I LOVE YOU in my bathroom, I had another area of my self-esteem God was helping me improve. That area was my body image. I thought my body was ugly, and I was ashamed of it. I used to walk with my shoulders down, trying to hide my body. A good friend of mine helped me by hitting me in the back every time he saw me in that position. He would say, "Walk tall and be proud of yourself." Needless to say, I developed a bruise on my shoulder! As I changed, I began to walk in an upright position and feel proud of myself, and I noticed my self-esteem began to improve.

"Beauty is in The Eye of the Beholder"

Around the same period I had to go to the Dominican Republic on a business trip. I used to think I had a big nose, and voiced this opinion to several friends in the Dominican Republic. A number of them began to tell me how pretty and perfect my nose was. Once again, I believe God was showing me I was okay just the way I was and beauty is in the eye of the beholder.

These three experiences made me realize that God was helping me love myself no matter what.

Many of us have tried to raise our self-esteem by changing our hair color, changing partners, moving to another location, or buying things to feel better. For a moment, we feel better, but soon we are back where we started, looking for the next change to achieve happiness.

We tell ourselves that if certain conditions would exist, we could be happy and feel good inside. The remedy for better self-esteem is to accept ourselves the way we are.

Happiness is an inside Job!

Take Responsibility for Your Self-esteem.

RESPONSIBILITY - the ability to respond properly. People with low self-esteem are afraid of responsibility because they do not feel they have the ability or the skills to respond properly to events in their lives.

Have you ever blamed someone else for what was happening in your life, or more importantly, blame someone else for how you feel, or blamed outside factors like the weather, the economy or your childhood?

STOP COMPLAINING, STOP BLAMING OTHERS - It is up to YOU to build your self-esteem. You are responsible for how you feel in any given situation. It is not about what anyone did to you; instead, it is about your interpretation of how you feel as a result of that action.

Self-esteem is an attitude toward ourselves that says:

1. I am responsible for myself.
2. I am responsible for identifying my needs (instincts) and my wants (desires)
3. I am responsible for my physical, emotional and spiritual well being
4. I am responsible for the choices and the risks I take in my life.
5. I am responsible for setting goals and achieving them.
6. I am responsible for how much I enjoy my life.
7. I am responsible for solving my problems.
8. I am responsible for what I do to others and myself.
9. I am responsible for how I feel at all times.
10. I am responsible for all the decisions I make.

11. I am responsible for my thoughts, feelings, and actions.
12. I am responsible for my life!

My life is what I make it!

Self-care is an attitude of self-respect. It means you are responsible for having your needs met.

Nurturing and Self-esteem

As children, to feel love and to feel lovable, we needed:

1. To have Nurturing --- Love
2. To have Structure

If you did not have these needs met as a child, you have to learn as an adult to nurture, love, and structure your life. Become responsible to meet your needs.

You have to become your own parent and give yourself:

1. Love
2. Nurturing
3. Structure
4. Discipline
5. Guidance (through mentors in your life, people who have what you want)
6. Encouragement and Support

Self-esteem is improved or damaged by the relationships we have in our lives.

Involve people in your life that will give you love, nurturing, guidance, encouragement, and support.

Toxic People and Self-esteem

Know the difference between nurturing people and toxic people.

Do you know people who walk into a room and everyone wants to leave? The reason is these people are negative or toxic.

Have you ever been with someone that leaves you feeling totally drained?

Toxic people are negative people and in order for them to feel better, they have to dump all of their negativism on someone else. They end up robbing other people's energy. Avoid these people if you want to improve your self-esteem.

SOMETIMES THE PEOPLE CLOSEST TO US, ARE UNFORTUNATELY, THE MOST TOXIC RELATIONSHIPS IN OUR LIVES.

In order for you to improve your self-esteem, you might need to create distance from some family member or friend who might be a toxic person.

Sometimes we want to avoid toxic people, but we feel we cannot. A friend of mine called me one day to tell me she did not want to go to her brother's house to celebrate her mother's birthday. One of the reasons was when her family got together they always put her down. Another reason was her financial level was not the same as the rest of the family. The most important reason was that they

Social Instinct – Relationship with Yourself and Relationship with Others

were very negative, and she always felt depressed after she left family reunions.

My reply to her was, "If you do not want to go, why don't you *follow your instinct* and not go?"

She said, "I have to go because it is my mother's birthday!"

"No, you do not have to go just because it is your mother's birthday," I replied. "If what you want is to celebrate your mother's birthday, why don't you ask her out to lunch, just the two of you, and that way you can stay away from the place that is toxic to you." I went on to say, "My suggestion is to be honest with your mother and express to her that you do not feel like going to the party, but that she is very important to you, and you would like to take her out to lunch and spend some quality time together."

My friend took her mother out to lunch and she did not have to go to the party where she was going to feel bad. As a result of her actions, she avoided the toxic people. She felt good about herself, improved the relationship with her mother, and improved her relationship with herself. She also increased her self-esteem and satisfied her social instinct.

My friend also set clear boundaries with her family. In the next chapter we are going to discuss the security instinct that has to do with establishing boundaries, and this will be further explained.

Knowing your needs (instincts) and satisfying them will help you create healthy results in every aspect of your life.

What is important about this situation is that my friend

was afraid to go to the party for fear of the messages she would receive. If she would have gone to the party, and received the usual negative messages, she would have felt badly. By choosing to take her mother out to lunch instead, she was able to establish clear boundaries for her wants (spend time with her mother on her birthday) and still satisfy her instincts (needs - not to expose herself to toxic people, her family).

THE TRUTH IS THAT NO ONE HAS THE POWER TO MAKE YOU FEEL BAD. Only YOU can make YOU feel bad.

Whenever I am in a situation or in a place where negativism is involved, I remove myself. I have an expression that says "Remove yourself from the unacceptable." Negativism is not acceptable in my life today. To me, *Negativism is a virus and is very contagious.*

It is Not What People Say to You. It is What You Say to Yourself that is Going to Determine How You Feel

If someone said to you, "You're stupid!" This message can only affect you if you accept the information. If you know you are not stupid, then why should someone else's opinion make you feel badly?
No one can make you feel bad without your permission.
When you have good self-esteem, the negative comments people tell you have no power and cannot affect you.
The solution to feeling good about yourself, regardless of what anyone else says, is to have good self-esteem.

Connect with who you are by connecting with your instincts.

One of the biggest challenges in my life has been to change what I imagine people think of me.

One time I was doing a seminar and one of my mentors was there. As soon as I finished, I rushed to him and asked him, "How do you think I did?"

He replied, "It is not important what I think. What is important is what you think of how you did!" This was one of the biggest lessons in my life. My mentor showed me with his actions and words that what I needed was to trust what I thought of myself.

Before, when my mentor did not tell me what I wanted to hear, I was very disappointed. I was waiting for a self-esteem boost like: "You did great; you were fantastic; you had a captive audience, and they were really paying attention to what you were saying." Later I understood I did not need to hear that information from him or anyone else. I needed to hear it from myself. I came to believe my mentor gave me a big gift - the gift of only looking inside myself for approval.

Still today, I have to be careful. As a child, I was programmed to believe what people thought of me was more important than what I thought of myself. I grew up in a family that always said, *"What are people going to think or say!"* I learned that what people thought and said about me was more important than what I thought and said about myself.

Today I still have to practice the following:

What people think or say about me is their business!

Follow Your Instincts

How about the people who walk in a room and everyone gets positive energy from them? Do you want to be that person, or the person that everyone avoids?

If you want to be the person everyone wants to talk to, all you have to do is improve your self-esteem and become positive. The better you think, and feel about who you are, and thus act, the more magnetic you will become to other people. The more you interact with positive people, the more your self-esteem will improve.

You can change how you think by choosing the messages you tell yourself. When you change your thinking, you will automatically change the way you feel, resulting in a new behavior.

If after I finished a seminar someone said to me that I was not a good speaker, that statement could make me feel bad about myself. I could accept it and feel bad, or I could change it by saying to myself, "I know I am a good speaker," and feel good.

Also, my performance is not who I am. What this means is that even if I perform poorly in a seminar that does not make me a bad speaker. It only means I did not perform as well as I could have. *I have to separate my performance from who I am.*

It is what you believe inside you to be true that is going to determine how you feel.

The Thought, Feeling, and Action Process

A thought creates a feeling and that feeling creates an action or behavior; then, that action or behavior reinforces, the original thought.

THOUGHT

↗   ↘

ACTION ← **FEELING**

Sometimes you can find yourself acting in a certain way, and you do not know how you got there. Be aware that a feeling precedes every action, and every feeling is preceded by a thought. If you want to know what feeling created your action, go back and figure out the thought that created the feeling. By changing the thought, you will change the feeling, and consequently, the action. Understanding this mechanism will empower you to change your life.

Everything you create in your life starts with a thought. For example, the last car you bought, the first thing you said or thought was, "I need to buy a car." Then, all of your actions took you in the direction of the purchase. You probably decided on the type of car you wanted before you even went out to look for one.

If at the time you thought of buying a new car, you said to yourself, "No, I do not deserve a new car," then, you would not have been able to purchase one.

It is important to notice the instinct involved in the car situation. If you have good self-esteem, and you have a good relationship with yourself, there is nothing wrong with buying a car. On the other hand, if you have low self-esteem and do not feel worthy of having a new car, you will begin to give yourself messages and reasons why you should not buy it. Has this ever happened to you? The better your self-esteem gets, the more you will feel worthy of receiving gifts, whether from yourself or others.

There is a saying:

You will continue to have what you always had, as long as you continue to think what you always thought.

Your Inner Dialogue

Start listening to yourself and constantly change your self-talk from <u>negative</u> to <u>positive</u>. It is important for you to learn to control and change your self-talk from negative to positive. The problem is trying to change is sometimes very difficult.

If you were programmed negatively as a child, you have to become aware your computer (mind) has a negative basis. It is up to you to create new positive programming with the power of affirmations. Understand your mind, unlike a computer, does not have a delete key. Consequently, you always have to be on the alert for that negative Self that might surface.

Your negative thoughts about yourself create low self-esteem. If you want good self-esteem, you have to stop the negative dialogue in your head. Be on constant guard not only of the messages you tell yourself, but also of the messages other people tell you.

Listen to your inside and outside messages. If someone

were to tell you you are a slow learner, and your instincts tell you the person is wrong, then, you say to yourself, "Cancel, cancel," and change the statement to a positive message, such as, "I am a fast learner." This is something you have to do all the time even when watching TV. Some commercials can be your worst enemy, giving you negative messages.

Some people think because they make a mistake, they are the mistake.

This is not so. If you make a mistake, all you have to do is learn from it and forgive yourself. Mistakes are necessary in the learning process. If you are too concerned about making mistakes, you are not going to be open to learn.

Sometimes it is difficult for you to find positive things to say to yourself.

My suggestion is to make a list of 50 positive qualities about yourself.

Ask your friends and family to help you make the list. Sometimes other people can see your qualities better than you can see them. Save this list and every time you are feeling you are not good enough, review it, use it to give positive messages to yourself.

If you have low self-esteem, making a list of 50 qualities about yourself might sound like a very big task. You might feel you do not have that many good qualities. Please be good to yourself and make this list. As soon as you make it, you will see yourself in a different light and your self-esteem will improve.

Follow Your Instincts

I have made a sample list to assist you:

1. I am positive
2. I am honest
3. I am loyal/faithful
4. I am reliable
5. I am a hard worker
6. I am determined
7. I am a good speaker
8. I am a good motivator
9. I do not gossip
10. I am a good friend
11. I am attractive
12. I am athletic
13. I have a great personality
14. I am kind
15. I am loving
16. I am caring
17. I am thankful
18. I am grateful
19. I am trustworthy
20. I am creative
21. I am organized
22. I am persistent
23. I am intuitive
24. I am spiritual
25. I am disciplined
26. I am sincere
27. I have fun in life
28. I have sense of humor
29. I am courageous
30. I am fair
31. I am thoughtful
32. I am a good listener
33. I am understanding
34. I am considerate
35. I am outgoing
36. I am elegant
37. I am dedicated
38. I am nurturing
39. I am sensitive
40. I am friendly
41. I am supportive
42. I am respectful
43. I am punctual
44. I am a leader
45. I have charisma
46. I am a great speaker
47. I am goal oriented
48. I am adventurous
49. I am persistent
50. I am a good wife/husband daughter/son mother/father, etc.

I could have easily made a list longer than 50 qualities; however, this is just a sample to assist you. I hope your list is much longer than 50 qualities.

It is important you look at the areas in your personality you need to change or improve. It is easier to look at your negative areas from a positive point of view. The list of your 50 qualities will help you accomplish that.

Many of us tend to look at the negative and not the positive, especially concerning ourselves. If your car has a bad generator, two bad tires, and it needs a paint job, it does not mean the car is not good. The same principle applies to people. Because a person may have a trait that needs to be changed, it does not make the person bad. It simply means the person has an area that needs improvement.

In the case of the car, it is important to notice that the three areas do not need to be corrected today. It is the same with people. We have to be loving and allow the other person to change whenever they are ready to grow at their own speed.

For years I looked for "normal" people, so that I could have role models. I came to the conclusion that normal people are hard to find. We all have areas that could be improved. I believe this is the reason God has placed us on this planet – *to learn and grow*.

I also came to the conclusion that I do not have to look for what is normal in other people, but to know what is normal for me. The way I succeed is by getting in touch with my instincts, and recognizing what is not normal in me, then working on getting it back to normal. It is my belief God placed instincts inside us as a road map to normality.

Follow Your Instincts

If you have:

Low self-esteem --- work on getting a healthy self-esteem, by loving yourself as you are unconditionally.

Another aspect of healthy self-esteem is not having the need to justify to ourselves or to others our treating ourselves nicely with things like: taking a vacation, buying new clothes, or simply spoiling ourselves from time to time.

Suggestions to Improve Your Self-esteem

1. Work on the physical
   a. Eat properly.
   b. Exercise.
   c. Get massages.
   d. Get proper amounts of rest.
   e. Take good care of your body. Have a physical every year, etc.
2. Work on the emotional
   a. Feel your feelings - get in touch with your emotions.
   b. Eliminate negative feelings like resentments, fears and guilt.
   c. Figure out which instincts are being affected, not satisfied, or those you are afraid will not be satisfied.
   d. Eliminate toxic people from your life.

3. Work on the spiritual
   Get in touch with your intuition, trust it, and follow it all the time. Meditation will get you in touch with your intuition.
4. Work on becoming positive
   a. Create a positive picture of yourself.
   b. Control your self-talk. Change it from negative to positive by using "cancel, cancel" after the negative statement and replace it with a positive statement.

Your thoughts create your attitude and your attitude will shape your life!

5. Stop looking for happiness in other people or things.
   Happiness is an inside job!
6. Stop looking for approval from others.
7. Value yourself and make decisions and choices that enhance your elf-esteem.
8. Examine the belief system that supports you. Make sure it is positive.
9. Stand up for yourself, your beliefs and values.
10. Learn to say NO, and realize that you do not need an explanation when you say no.
11. Stop comparing yourself to others.
12. Take risks -- be willing to get out of your comfort zone.
13. Don't take yourself too seriously --- *Laugh at yourself.*
14. Stop negativism.

Follow Your Instincts

15. Concentrate on what you can do and do it now.
16. Stop worrying. Take action.
17. Find out what your needs are and fulfill them.
18. Start each day by being grateful to be here --- it is a new day – a new opportunity.

Building Your Self-esteem is Going to Take Time

There is a tree in Asia called Bamboo. To grow this tree you must plant the seed, fertilize it, and water it every day for 5 years. During the five-year period, nothing occurs. You do not even see a shoot of the tree. Then, some day, about five years later, the tree will grow about 9 feet in about 5 weeks.

My question to you is: How long does it take the Bamboo tree to grow, 5 weeks or 5 years?

The answer of course is 5 years.

The same thing happens to your self-esteem. Sometimes you will be working on yourself for a very long time, and you may feel there is no progress. However, like the Bamboo tree, one day when you least expect it, you will begin to shine.

TAKE TIME TO WORK ON YOU! *You are the most precious gift you will ever have.*

Beware of Television and the Movies

Television can become a terrible enemy by creating in us a false image of ourselves. Whenever I saw the perfect family on television, sharing Christmas and exchanging gifts around the Christmas tree, I used to get depressed. I wanted the perfect family like the one I was being shown

Social Instinct – Relationship with Yourself and Relationship with Others

on TV. I used to think something was wrong with me.

When the movie ends, the beautiful people live happily ever after (the perfect relationship -- the prince on the white horse). Relationships are not perfect. People are not perfect. When I came to that conclusion, I was able to have a healthy relationship in my life. Before, I was always looking for that perfect man who did not exist, and if he did, why would he want me?

This does not mean you should lower your standards when looking for a mate; it just means you realistically look for a compatible and loving lifetime partner.

It is easier for us to be more tolerant of others when we are able to accept our own imperfections.

Look for the positive in yourself as well as in other people and express it. *There is always something positive to tell yourself and others.*

Benjamin Franklin's Rule

When you are trying to figure out certain aspects of your life, it is a good idea to use Benjamin Franklin's Rule, which is to take a piece of paper, draw a line down the middle and put the positive attributes on one side and the negative on the other. This will allow you to create a balance between the negative and the positive before you make a decision.

POSITIVE   NEGATIVE

Follow Your Instincts

If you are trying to figure out if a person is toxic for you, Ben's Rule can be very helpful when applied to that person.

The reason you want to stay away from toxic people and surround yourself with positive ones is that at the instinct level you know the positive person is going to help raise your self-esteem.

I use the Benjamin Franklin Rule in my business. If I see that it might be necessary to fire someone, before I actually take action, I review the positive and negative traits of that person. If there are more positives than negatives, I might have a meeting with that person and suggest some changes. In many cases, I actually have not had to let that employee go.

In friendships, it is also very helpful to use this method before you start or end a relationship. Sometimes I can be quick to judge a person. Ben's Rule prevents me from being unfair with other people.

2. Relationships with Other People

Relationships with other people are the result of your interactions. As you interact with others you are satisfying the following two areas:

    a. FRIENDSHIP -- Friendship is to feel capable of having friends and being one; to be welcome, to be accepted, to feel you belong, to have companionship and to be capable of being part of a fellowship or a community.

    b. PRESTIGE -- Prestige is a feeling that you are recognized, successful, valuable, important,

Social Instinct – Relationship with Yourself and Relationship with Others

contributing, useful, respected, reputable, and that you have leadership capabilities as a result of your interaction with other people.

Feelings

Emotions are feelings in motion. That is it. They are not good or bad, they just are.

You have to acknowledge your emotions. If you feel bad about your emotions, you are going to lower your self-esteem.

THERE ARE ONLY FOUR BASIC FEELINGS (emotions)

1. MAD
2. SAD
3. GLAD
4. SCARED

Give yourself permission to feel them. Everything else is a thought.

You have to allow yourself to feel feelings in order to connect with your instincts. Get into the habit of saying to yourself, "Why is it I feel this way?" For instance, if you feel sad, which instinct is not satisfied, or do you think will not be satisfied? If you are happy, what instinct is satisfied? This way you can start connecting with your instincts.

Follow Your Instincts

Sometimes you may get mad (angry), then you feel bad about being so. Maybe as a child you were told you should not feel anger, and you began to become disconnected from your instincts.

Let's say you say to yourself: "She makes me mad (angry)." The truth is she does not have the power to make you angry. You make yourself angry! Remember, what we discussed before in this chapter: you control your thoughts. The only way to not give your power away is to be in touch with your instincts and follow them. As you learn to express your emotions, your self-esteem will improve, and you will feel good about yourself.

Do Not Give Your Power Away

Every time you give your power to another person, you lower your self-esteem. The reason is you are saying to yourself the other person's opinion or actions are more important than yours.

You have not given your power away when a fireman says, "Jump out of the window, or you will burn to death." The reason you follow his instructions is because you agree with them.

Have You Ever Made a Geographical Move, Hoping Your Life Will Change, or Do You Know Someone Who Has?

People who make a geographical change think their situation will change if they are in a different place. The problem is they take themselves wherever they go!

Social Instinct – Relationship with Yourself and Relationship with Others

Many people believe a change of environment will change them, but in reality, if they have low self-esteem, they end up taking it with them.

If you have low self-esteem and feel bad about yourself, it does not matter where you go, you will still feel that way because feeling good or bad about yourself is something you create.

Happiness is an inside job!

Once you change how you feel inside, your outside world will change. There is no need to go anywhere. You can be happy right here, right now. All it takes is for you to connect with your God given instincts!

What About Values?

Every time you do something that conflicts with your values, you lower your self-esteem.

If your belief is to be faithful (your value), and you are unfaithful (your action), the result is you feel guilty. To achieve peace you have to either change your actions or change your belief.

It is easier to change the action than to change your belief. Changing your belief is much more challenging, but can produce greater rewards.

Some people would rather be confused about their values than decide what their values are because while they are confused about their values, they do not have to take action.

Confusion is a great way to avoid responsibility!

Have you ever been in a situation where you have compromised your integrity and felt terrible about it afterwards?

The reason is that at an instinctual level you know you should not compromise your integrity under any circumstances. However, at the intellectual level you may not be very clear about your values.

When you compromise your integrity, you sacrifice your values and the message you give yourself is that you are not important and you are not good. This behavior will lower your self-esteem.

When you have a clear set of values, it is easy to have self-respect. One of the objectives of this book is to provide the tools to examine your values and perhaps create a new set for yourself.

How About Comparing Yourself with Others?

Comparing yourself to someone else will cause misery. Do not do it!

Have you ever tried to change someone such as your husband or wife, or your significant other, only to get frustrated?

The only thing you can change is how you react to what they do.

Comfort Zone

To improve your self-esteem, you must experience life. Sometimes that includes rejection. You have to take chances, take risks, and get out of your comfort zone.

In order to learn, you have to participate. Some people choose isolation as a way to avoid participating. You do not learn a game unless you play. Life is the same way. You do not learn unless you play. Get involved and participate.

IF YOU WANT YOUR LIFE TO CHANGE, YOU HAVE TO CHANGE

You have to be willing to get out of your comfort zone in order for your life to change. Your comfort zone, a place with which you are familiar and where you feel comfortable, safe and secure, is not an easy place to leave.

To take a risk you have to get out of your comfort zone. Do you have to get out of your comfort zone when you ask someone to lunch? For some people the answer is yes. If you ask someone out to lunch, and they say "no," it does not matter. Your situation is just the same as it was before you asked them. You still have yourself to go to lunch with. Did your situation get worse? No. Then why are we so afraid of asking people? Again, because of fear of rejection. It would be crazy to continue to eat alone for fear of rejection. Why not take a risk and ask someone to lunch?

Insanity is to continue to do the same thing and expect different results.

It is important to know that your comfort zone may keep you from getting to where you want to go. You have to get out of your comfort zone if you want to accomplish something different.

Follow Your Instincts

Taking risks forces you to get out of your comfort zone. The more risks you take the more experiences you will accumulate and the easier it will become. Knowing you are capable of getting out of your comfort zone will help you develop self-confidence, which in turn will help you develop higher self-esteem.

Do you know why the golf ball has so many indentations?

When the golf ball was first created it was round with no indentations. As the game developed, the golfers discovered that when the golf ball had indentations it could go father than a new smooth ball. Golfers began to study how many indentations were necessary for the golf ball to go the farthest. This is how we arrived at the golf ball we have today.

By taking risks you are creating indentations in yourself, hence making yourself stronger to deal with life. The importance of getting out of your comfort zone is that it does not matter if the risks you take have positive or negative results. What matters is the experience you will obtain as a result of taking that risk.

My message to you is to become like a golf ball. Create so many experiences that you will be able to flow with life.

The more you take risks and become willing to get out of your comfort zone, the more courage you will have, the further you will go in life.

Let me ask you a question. When you go to a party, who do you socialize with? Usually someone you know, right? The reason is that is your comfort zone, and rejection from those you know is most unlikely.

Have you been tempted to, or actually cancelled going to a party because you thought no one you knew would be there? Have you thought about missing the opportunity of meeting new people? Would you like to enjoy new experiences rather than fear them? If you continue with your present behavior, then what?

If you keep doing what you have always done, you will keep getting what you always got.

Fake It Until You Make It

Sometimes in life in order to get out of your comfort zone, you have to fake it until you make it!

I remember one time, I did not have an income. I was in debt, the bank was ready to repossess my car, and everyone was calling me for money. The reason I was going through this period was that I had just spent over nine months in a foreign country working on a business deal that did not materialize. I was feeling like a failure, not feeling very good about myself, and needless to say my self-esteem was really low.

I badly needed cash flow and a good friend of mine referred me to a bank that was looking for someone to manage several properties, including a shopping center. He made an appointment for me with the president of the bank. At that time in my life, I was intimidated by what I call the "authority figures," especially if they were older than me. My friend indicated that the president of the bank was an elderly gentleman. This information intimidated me.

When the appointment day arrived, I asked God for help because I knew my self-esteem was very low, and I needed to go there with the right attitude. In spite of how I was feeling, I put the "fake it, until you make it" expression to good use; thus, I went to my appointment feeling like a million dollars. I was faking it!

At the appointment, I was sitting in front of five men who intimidated me, and the president asked me, "Tell me a good reason why I should contract you?"

"With all due respect sir," I answered, "you cannot afford to not use my services because I am simply the best!"

I said this statement with so much conviction, that he immediately replied, "You're hired."

I negotiated a wonderful deal. I faked it, and I made it! The result of this meeting was that my self-esteem immediately increased, and I felt very good about myself.

Winners are people who make a habit of doing the things that losers are uncomfortable doing!

It is not that the winner does not experience fear; it is that the winner will continue in spite of the fear.

Do you think I was afraid at my appointment with the president of the bank? Absolutely, but I did it anyway!

Failure is Part of Success

"Courage is going from failure to failure without losing enthusiasm." — Winston Churchill

The more you risk, the more you are going to fail. The more you fail, the more you are going to learn. Failure is part of the learning process. *Failure is part of success.*

Maybe at one time you, like myself, felt if you failed that made you a failure. This kind of mentality will prevent you from getting out of your comfort zone and taking risks.

IF YOU HAD A FAILURE THAT DOES NOT MAKE YOU A FAILURE!

Give yourself the opportunity to investigate life. If you fail at something, make it an experience in life's journey, and not a failure. This attitude will help you take more risks.

Success is a journey, not a destination

Sometimes in life you might have a desire to take a risk, and get out of your comfort zone, but you cannot get motivated. To help you get motivated I have a formula:

NEED + FAITH = MOTIVATION
(the belief you can do it)

Your NEED, coupled with FAITH will MOTIVATE you (perhaps to get out of your comfort zone and take risks).

The Universe rewards action. Become an active participant in life by always being willing to take risks, and get out of your comfort zone.

Sometimes life hits us hard and we fail so many times that it is very difficult to be willing to take more risks. Sometimes what we end up doing is focusing on the failures instead of on our successes. My suggestion to you is to make a list of all your successes, so the next time you have to take a risk, you will find encouragement from seeing how many times you have succeeded in the past.

Increase Your Self-esteem by Knowing Your Life's Purpose

Another way to increase your self-esteem is by getting in touch with your life's purpose. When you feel you have a reason for being, it makes you feel good about yourself.

Example: Being a mother or father.
Being a teacher, a healer, etc.
Helping an addict get into recovery (service).

Ask yourself this question:

What are two unique qualities that I have? Somewhere within these qualities is your life purpose.

Example:
I am nurturing --- Maybe your life purpose is to be a mother or father, or perhaps a teacher.
I am organized and structured --- Maybe your life purpose is to help businesses get organized, and have your own business in the process.
I love to listen to people's problems --- Maybe your life purpose is to be a counselor.

What Makes Your Personality or Your Identity?

Your personality and identity are those attributes that include your talents, abilities, limitations, fears, conflicts and memories of your past. This is why it is so important to really study yourself and get to know you. The better you know yourself, the better you will function in society and the better social skills you will have.

According to the dictionary, identity is:

1. To recognize or establish one's self as being a particular person.
2. The condition of being one's self and not another.
3. The state or fact of remaining the same under varying aspects or conditions.
4. Oneness.
5. Unity and persistence of personality; individuality.

Community Involvement -- Social Instinct

The more familiar you become with your social instinct, the better social skills you will have. The social instinct allows us to have a relationship with ourselves and to live in society (part of a group).

My husband fell from a ladder and broke his leg. During that period, a group we belong to was praying for him. One day, after his leg was better, we arrived at the meeting and a young woman from the group we did not know came up to us and said, "You are the Bob that we have been praying for. It is nice to associate a face with the person, but more importantly, it was a new experience for me to be part of the community and pray for someone I did not know. It made me feel good."

Follow Your Instincts

The reason Maria felt good praying for someone who belonged to her group was that she satisfied her social instinct.

Stand Up For Yourself

Why is it that sometimes you do not stand up for yourself?

Because of low self-esteem, you probably end up "people pleasing." You do not want to hurt the other person's feelings, so who do you end up hurting? That's right, yourself.

When we "people please" and we want to be the "nice person," we often allow people to push our buttons or instincts. The primary reason for this behavior is low self-esteem. When you respect yourself enough you do not allow anyone to push your buttons. If you set boundaries and they get upset, so what!

You give your power away when:

1. You people please and allow others to push your buttons.

2. Look for other's approval because of low self-esteem.

Self-esteem and personal relations are interconnected. You cannot affect one without affecting the other.

LEARN TO BECOME YOUR OWN BEST FRIEND!
STOP PEOPLE PLEASING.
THE RESULT WILL BE INCREASED SELF-ESTEEM.

Start and Finish Tasks

Another important issue of low self-esteem is not finishing things that get started. Usually people with low self-esteem start but do not finish.

It is very important to do what I call "close cycles." This means to start and finish things. Closing cycles will assist you in becoming more self-confident and improve your self-esteem in the process.

There might be different reasons why you do not finish things, and they may be:

1. That you get bored with the process of doing a task.
2. That something else comes up that looks more interesting.
3. You simply have a habit of doing many things at once.

Whatever the reason, when you have a lot of projects going at the same time, a small part of your mind is in every project, and you are fragmented.

Learn to start and finish things. Work on one project at a time. That way you can focus and direct your energy better. People with high self-esteem start and finish things.

If you really want to build your self-esteem, you have to become aware of every action you take and how this action will affect you. Always maintain integrity with yourself at all costs!

Integrity is the fastest way to improve and raise your self-esteem.

Developing Friendships

You have to become your own best friend by spending time with yourself, trusting yourself, honoring your decisions, keeping your word (if I speak it I will do it), accepting yourself with the good and the bad, and loving yourself unconditionally. Once you have a good relationship with yourself, then you can develop a good relationship with other people.

To develop a friendship with someone takes time. You have to give of yourself, give time, energy, have patience and be caring and loving. You have to respect the other person's opinion even if it is different than yours. In other words, in order to respect the other person as an individual, you have to trust and, most importantly, love that person with the good and the bad.

It is important to know you do not have to be everyone's friend. Choose as friends people who are nurturing and loving to you.

Dog's Friendship

Dogs are man's best friend, but they are also best friends to each other. I would like to share with you the story of the three dogs that came to my office.

I was at my office and three dogs came to the front door. They looked like a happy trio. A man came in a van and asked me if these dogs were mine, and if not, he wanted to take one of them home. The dog he wanted looked similar to one his family had lost a few months before, and he felt that his son would be very happy to have a dog again. Thinking of the little boy, I said, "I think it will be okay."

The man proceeded to take one of the dogs.

A few minutes after the man left, the other two dogs became desperate, looking for their friend. They kept going up and down the street looking for him. You could almost feel their pain. When I saw this, I realized I should not have allowed the man to take the dog, but it was too late.

This incident helped me realize dogs are not only man's best friend, but they are also dog's best friend. Animals act on pure instinct. These dogs were manifesting the social instinct.

Losing a friend is painful. Why should we think dogs do not have the same feelings? Actually, they show it better than we do.

Companionship and friendly association is part of the social instinct. These dogs were showing me they were missing their buddy. We have so much to learn from animals! They can be our teachers. I believe we can learn how to be friends, similar to the dogs, by using our God-given instinct.

Companionship is part of the social instinct, and we need it to be healthy human beings.

Social Instinct and Animals

We have much to learn from animals about companionship. I have a neighborhood cat that comes to the kitchen glass door for me to feed him. He sometimes stays by the glass door just to keep me company. I noticed one day when I moved to the living room the cat also moved to the living room's sliding glass door, close enough to give and feel companionship.

Another day, when I was feeding the neighborhood cats, I noticed a bird was watching, and as soon as they finished, it took advantage of their departure and called other birds to the remaining feast. The bird's social instinct caused it to call the others. The bird, at an instinct level, knows that she must help the rest of the flock to survive, thus ensuring her own survival.

Another example of the social instinct used for self-preservation is when in a group of monkeys, one monkey notices danger and alerts the rest of the group. This is true of all animals that live in groups.

Man is a Social Being

Have you ever been alone in your house and had the need to call some friend to visit? This again is the social instinct (relationship with others). We need people. We need the community.

I was watching a TV show about two groups of ten people that were supposed to compete on an isolated island. Every week they had different challenges and the group that lost would have to vote a member out. After a few weeks there were only 5 in each group and now the challenge was to unite, forming a new group that could exist in harmony. The interesting part was that everyone interviewed wanted to unite, to feel part of a bigger community. The larger the group, the more opportunity there is to satisfy the social instinct.

Isolation will keep you from satisfying the social instinct. You need interaction to satisfy the social instinct.

Social Instinct – Relationship with Yourself and Relationship with Others

We Need Others in Our Lives.

One day I was having lunch with a friend of mine, Lulu, who lives in the Dominican Republic. Lulu began to tell me she was having difficulties remembering things. I suggested vitamins. She said she did not need them because she knew what was happening to her. Lulu went on to explain that as a result of working on her beach project, she was not socializing. The only people available to speak to were her employees, who she did not have very much in common with. Her conversations were limited to instructions.

As a result of not interacting with others, Lulu was not satisfying her social instinct as part of a community, and her isolation was slowing her thinking process. We both realized that she needed to get her mind active again, and she needed more satisfying interaction. She went back to the Dominican Republic and began to interact more with neighbors, and her thinking process, as well as her memory improved tremendously.

Make Someone's Day

Another way to satisfy the social instinct is to see the good in people and let them know it. Go ahead, make their day!

On my way to work I used to pass by a tollbooth. Every day I would get a receipt from this lady that seemed to be upset all the time. I made it my job to make her day every day. I would go by her booth at 7:00 am and say in a very enthusiastic tone, "Good morning!" She never responded. I continued to do the same for one month and finally, one day, I heard, "Good morning to you too." My immediate reaction was to say, "Great, now I am going to work on your smile!" She laughed and ever since then, she has shown a positive attitude.

I believe you can influence people around you. If you are positive and good with people wherever you go, you might make someone's day!

Compliments

Giving as well as accepting compliments is part of the social instinct.

Accepting compliments is connected to your self-image and your self-esteem. For me, learning to accept compliments was one of the most difficult things I had to do. Every time someone complimented me about something I was wearing, I would say something like, "It's an old dress." Or, "I only paid $ _____ for it." I would say something to indicate the compliment was not necessary. The truth was that I did not feel worthy of a compliment. Finally, I learned to just say "Thank you" without any explanation and accept the compliment.

When I get a compliment now, I know I am allowing the other person to be nice to me, and at the same time give them an opportunity to satisfy their social instinct. Who am I to deprive them of that?

When I realized that giving and receiving compliments is part of satisfying my social instinct, I began to give them more often. The more I complimented others, the more compliments I received. Today, it is easier for me to give and receive.

A compliment is a gift. It takes thought and energy.

Social Instinct – Relationship with Yourself and Relationship with Others

When you give a gift, it is very disappointing if the person does not want to accept it. Thus, it is important to accept a compliment gracefully with a thank you.

SUMMARY

The social instinct is the interaction you have with other people and most importantly, the relationship you have with yourself. It is composed of two parts: relationship with yourself and relationship with others.

Relationship with Yourself

You have to become your own best friend by spending time with yourself, trusting yourself, honoring your decisions, keeping your word, accepting yourself with the good and the bad, and more importantly, loving yourself unconditionally. The relationship you have with yourself is connected to your self-esteem. It includes:

a. SELF-RESPECT
Self-respect is expressed by how you value yourself, how think of yourself, our own sense of dignity, and more importantly, how you love yourself.

b. PRIDE
Pride is a sense of feeling good about yourself. It is feeling good about your work and what you do, feeling good about your achievements and accomplishments.

Self-esteem is the way you see and value yourself. It includes being able to respect and love yourself. It is a sense of feeling proud about who you are. High self-esteem could be described as your ability to feel lovable and capable.

Your self-esteem manifests itself in every area of your life, such as your relationship with yourself, your relationship with others, and your relationships with your work and social activities.

People with high self-esteem are happy people who love their lives. They capitalize on their strengths to produce the results they want.

Once you have a good relationship with yourself, you are able to have good relationships with others.

Relationships with Others

Relationships with other people are the result of your interactions. As you interact with others you are satisfying the following two areas:

    a. FRIENDSHIP
    Friendship is feeling capable of having friends and being one; being welcome, accepted and feeling that you belong, having companionship and being part of a fellowship or a community.

    b. PRESTIGE
    Prestige is a feeling that you are recognized, successful, valuable, important, contributing, useful, respected, reputable, and that you have leadership capabilities as a result of your interaction with other people.

Social Instinct – Relationship with Yourself and Relationship with Others

As you develop relationships with other people, it is important to remember nurturing versus toxic people. Stay away from toxic, negative people. Embrace people in your life who are nurturing, loving, and supportive.

The social instinct is feeling capable of having good relationships with yourself and others, and being a contributing part of society.

Embrace life and spend time working on you. Know you are the best gift the Creator gave you!

You deserve to be happy, healthy, and have the things you want in life!

If civilization is to survive, we must cultivate the signs of human relationships – the ability of all people, of all kinds, to live together in the same world at peace.

- Franklin D. Roosevelt

Chapter 3

SECURITY INSTINCT – SELF-PRESERVATION AND COMMUNICATION

What is Security Instinct?

Security instinct has to do with self-preservation and communication.

Security instinct has to do with self-preservation by seeking food, shelter, clothing and personal space. It is also your ability to communicate with others. The security instinct is composed of two parts: self-preservation and communication.

1. Self-Preservation

Self-preservation pertains to physical and non-physical well-being.

PHYSICAL - food, shelter, clothing, health aids, money as a medium of exchange, and personal space.

It is easy for you to understand the need for food, shelter, and health aids. However, as far as money and personal space are concerned, there is tremendous confusion. Entire books have been written on these two subjects. My intent is to explain them as clearly as possible. Money, as a medium of exchange, is so important that I have dedicated an entire chapter to this subject (see Chapter 9, Connect with Your Instincts - Connect with Wealth).

Personal Space (part of self-preservation)

Boundaries in geography are borders defining a piece of land. One of the ways mankind has felt the need to mark their territory or boundary is by the use of fences. It is a way of creating privacy as well as preventing aggression. If your property has clearly defined areas by the use of fences, you are saying, "No trespassing." You are giving a fair warning. It is part of your security instinct to feel safe.

In the animal kingdom (of which we humans are a part) boundaries are the limits that establish territory or personal space.

Personal space is the area where you end and the other person begins.

We have personal space in three areas:
1. Physical
2. Emotional
3. Spiritual

1. Physical Space

Physical space has to do with your body, the space

where you end and someone else begins.

The best way to describe personal space is for you to imagine you are in an elevator at the first floor, and you are the only person in that elevator. What is your personal space or territory? The answer, of course, is the full elevator. Now imagine the elevator stops at the second floor and one person enters. What is your personal space now? Of course, half the elevator. Then the elevator continues moving up and stops on the third floor and two more people enter. What is your personal space now? One fourth the elevator. I think you get my point!

The problem with a lot of us is that we do not adjust our personal space as may be necessary and this gets us in a lot of trouble. Imagine, if in the elevator example, you would have been upset when another person entered the elevator because you felt they took some of your personal space. Would that attitude cause you a problem? I think so. What happens with personal space for some of us is that on some occasions we do not know what our space is, and on other occasions, we might just want more than we are entitled to.

Another example is when you enter a doctor's office. Sometimes it takes you a few minutes to figure out where you are going to sit. Does it not?

Have you ever sat in a chair too close to someone else? Maybe you felt uncomfortable because the other chair was too close to you. Maybe you felt you did not have enough personal space. We have all, at one time or another had the experience of feeling too close to another person. The reason is that at an instinctual level we all have the same information inside us.

Do you know someone whose home was robbed? Did they feel violated? The reason they did is because their personal space was violated!

Our physical space (boundaries) is violated when someone touches us without our permission. This is why it is a good idea if you are going to hug someone to always ask for his or her permission first.

Possession – Part of Your Personal Space

Health aids are part of your personal space. When I was a little girl I wanted to have my own hairbrush, but I could not, because in my family there was a belief that we needed to share everything. On one of my birthdays my uncle gave me a hairbrush. I was so happy! Finally I could satisfy my instinct. However, my family kept telling me that I needed to share my hairbrush with other members of my family. When I refused, I was told that I was being selfish, and as a result I felt ashamed.

For years I continued to feel I should have the right to my own hairbrush (satisfy my instinct - health aids, personal space). My family was telling me one thing and I was feeling something different. As a result, I began to disconnect from my instincts. For years I felt guilty and ashamed for feeling this way. It was not until later, when I became enlightened, that I realized I was right. My instinct was telling me I had the right to my own personal space and belongings, including my hairbrush.

The objective of this book is to help you reconnect with your instincts. If you have any unresolved incidents from your childhood, you can find serenity through understanding.

Security Instinct – Self-Preservation and Communication

When your intellect has information that's different from your instincts, you become fragmented. Alignment of intellect and instincts makes you feel whole.

Animals Know Their Personal Space

I have a security dog, a German Shepherd (Champ), I take with me to work every morning. He sits behind my desk in the office. That area is his personal space. He does not even allow the cleaning lady to move him.

A cat showed up at the office and we decided to adopt him. We created a space in the back office for the cat. The dog does not go to the back office. He knows the cat is there, and the cat does not come to the front office to invade his space. Each one respects the other's space instinctively.

For office security, a few months later, I adopted two Rottwieler dogs. My personal security dog was showing signs of what I thought was jealousy. I realized the dog was showing fear of losing his possession (me) and/or his position as a protector.

Fear is a gift from God as a mechanism for self-preservation (I will discuss fear at length in Chapter 7). My dog was afraid his personal space was going to be affected. His fear was his security instinct at work. Also, Champ was afraid the love I gave him was going to be shared with another dog. As soon as he realized everything was the same, his demand for more time and attention stopped. Haven't you seen humans do the same?

Another example of personal space: When a dog uses his nose to analyze another dog's urine, and then urinates on top of it, he is establishing his territory. He is establishing personal space by saying to the other dog: "This space is mine and you are now notified."

What Makes a Dog Bark?

A dog's bark is an instinctive reaction to surprise and a call for help to protect his personal space. This is part of its security as well as its social instinct. When he growls he is exhibiting his security instinct and saying, at this instant he is prepared to defend his personal space himself, but may call for help later. Calling for the rest of the pack for help is part of the social instinct.

Comparing the behavior of dogs and humans, we can see the similarities.

What a person is saying when expressing anger is, "I feel attacked and I will protect myself."

Animals act on pure instinct. Any time someone invades their personal space, they will protect it. In the wild, guarding your personal space is a matter of survival. Then why don't we, as part of the animal kingdom, guard our personal space more carefully?

The reason is that many times we have not defined our own personal space, and even if it is known, we do not assertively protect it.

Animals that live in packs do so to guarantee the survival of their species. Having shared personal space, they alert each other of possible danger, thus ensuring their survival.

Knowing our limitations can be helpful in establishing our boundaries. Because getting enough rest is very important to me, when I do not get the required amount I become irritable. Even when I go on vacation with my

Security Instinct – Self-Preservation and Communication

husband (who needs less rest than I do), I have to set boundaries.

We recently visited Las Vegas, a city that never sleeps, and my husband wanted to go and do things, but I needed my rest. I told him, "You can go down to the casino while I rest." I was able to set boundaries as a result of being in touch with my instincts.

2. Emotional Space

Emotional space has to do with your feelings and emotions. You have to become aware of what is acceptable to you. You have to know your values, and what you will accept from others.

Our emotional personal space is affected when we are criticized, or any time a negative statement is directed toward us.

Emotional pain is a message that we might need to set a boundary, or an indicator that we need to change the way we see things.

Pain (either physical or emotional) is a warning signal that we should change direction. Example: In the physical, if you place your hand on a hot stove, the pain is the message to do something about correcting it - *quickly!*

In the emotional, negative criticisms bring about another type of pain, and it could be a message to change.

3. Spiritual Space

You have a spiritual energy inside you that combines with your surrounding energy (sometimes referred to as the aura). Becoming familiar with these energies will allow you to set boundaries. Your spiritual belief becomes part of your spiritual space. An Italian friend explained karma to me in this simple way:

"You do good ---- you get good back!
You do bad ---- you get bad back!"

Because I believe this theory, I cannot allow anyone to pressure me to go against my moral values.

Boundaries

When setting boundaries, you have to be aware. You have to set them in the three areas described: physical, emotional, and spiritual.

You need to know how far you can go, and how far you will allow others to go with you. Identifying your personal space will enable you to establish boundaries.

Most of us have a hard time defining where we end, and another person begins, because of not being in touch with our God-given instincts.

Setting boundaries, a skill that can be learned and developed, means settings limits.

Your personal space is instinctively created, and I will assist you in setting proper boundaries later in the assertiveness chapter.

Some of us have to work harder at setting boundaries than others, and that is okay!

You set boundaries or limits when you are ready, and you will do it in your own time.

If you have never set boundaries before, you probably feel you do not have the right to do so. *This is not correct!*

Instincts are God-given, which means that you have the right to feel them regardless of what anyone might think. When you are faced with a feeling, it is important to understand that it is not good or bad. A feeling is just a feeling, and it is your right to set the proper boundary. While it is your right to set boundaries, we also have the responsibility of not hurting others when establishing them.

Each one of us has a built-in manual, a guide that lets us know about our boundaries (or personal space) called — INSTINCTS.

It is not necessary to keep your guard up all the time, but you should pay attention and be aware of any intrusion into your territory.

You need to feel safe in getting your life's needs met, including the setting of boundaries. God always supplies your needs, just as God supplies food for the birds, but does not put it in their nest! You are the one who has to connect with them.

Part of setting boundaries is being capable of saying "no." When saying "no," you can still care for the other person and feel safe in doing so.

How Can You Tell If a Boundary Is Affected?

You can tell a boundary has been affected when you hear yourself complaining, or when you see yourself get angry, a boundary may have been affected.

Anger is good; it might be telling you exactly what is wrong! We have been trained to believe anger is bad, but it is a feeling that God uses to alert us something is not right.

What is important is how you behave when you experience the anger.

Anger is usually an indicator that your instincts have been affected, or are being affected, and you might have to set a boundary.

Anger and resentment will be discussed in Chapter 6.

Boundary Area Awareness

What areas do you have to look at in order to know what boundaries you may have to set?

1. What hurts?
2. What feels good?
3. What are the responsibilities that you have – especially with yourself?
4. What are you willing to lose or not lose?

When you need to set a limit with someone, it works best to do it clearly and in as few words as possible, preferably without anger. If you are going to set a boundary and you are upset, it is a good idea to wait for a cooling-off period.

You may feel afraid and perhaps guilty when you set a boundary, or when you say "no." That's okay. Feel the guilt! I will guarantee the feeling of guilt will pass. As you set healthy boundaries for yourself, your self-esteem will increase, and the guilt eventually will disappear. What happens, if you have never set boundaries, is that you are getting out of your comfort zone, and that is uncomfortable. The more you set boundaries, the easier it will be.

Sometimes we have to set boundaries, and we don't for fear of hurting the other person. The result will be a lower self-esteem, because you are placing the other person before yourself. For me, that is a high price to pay!

Demanding Respect for One's Time

I would like to share with you my nail appointment story:

I always have my nails done in a beauty salon that respects my time. If my appointment is for 2:00 p.m., they take care of me at 2:00 p.m.

The lady who does my nails told me that sometimes the receptionist books people between appointments. That sets back the regular customers and causes her tension.

One day, I arrived at my appointment time, and someone was just beginning to get her nails done. This meant I would have to wait for an additional half-hour. Having a party that evening, I did not want to go without having my nails done. I waited to have my manicure and afterwards was feeling terrible. It took a few hours for me to realize I allowed my *instinct* to be affected. My time (as a boundary) was not respected.

After meditating about what happened, I came to the conclusion that because I did not say anything about being upset concerning my appointment at the beauty salon, I allowed the emotional part of the security instinct to get affected. As a result of not standing up for myself, and having respect for my time, my self-esteem was affected.

After I arrived at the above conclusion, I said to myself *"the next time something like this happens, I am going to stand up for myself. Receiving this kind of treatment is not acceptable; I respect other people's time and mine should be respected also."*

Follow Your Instincts

My husband planned to take me to a fancy restaurant for our anniversary. I wanted to look my best, so I made an appointment to have my nails done. Upon arrival at the beauty salon, at my appointment time, again, the manicurist was with a customer. I asked the receptionist, "Is that lady just starting to get her nails done?"

"Yes," she replied.

Without giving her any explanations, I walked out of the salon. I figured that if they did not take the time to explain, I owed them no explanation for leaving.

Sometimes actions speak louder than words. My actions spoke for me. Although my reaction was somewhat harsh, I felt better because now my self-esteem was lifted and my relationship with myself was improved. I was proud of myself.

When I relayed this story to my husband to explain why my nails were not done, he said, "I am very proud of you for standing up for yourself." That was all I needed to feel pretty that evening.

The next time I went to the salon, I thought the manicurist or the receptionist would say something, but no one said a word. Ever since that day, my appointments are respected, and if they are going to be even five minutes late, they call me to let me know.

Respect is Yours to Have

On another occasion my husband and I won some money on one of those one-day cruises. We decided to reward ourselves and buy some items we wanted for the house, which included a television set for the kitchen, a treadmill to replace the one we had, and we had agreed to save the balance to buy a big screen television for the family room.

Security Instinct – Self-Preservation and Communication

We went to a trendy sport store to purchase a treadmill. While at the store, one of the employees tried to sell us the display machine. I did not want to buy a used one. I acted assertively and I said, "I only want a new one." I suggested he call their other stores to see if they had a new one in stock. The attendant agreed and went to make some phone calls.

An hour later, the attendant returned and said he had located one, and all we needed to do was to place the order. I said, "Okay, we would like to pay for it so we can go." The attendant still made us wait another half hour.

What made me even more upset was that our salesman, together with another salesman, were attending a newly arrived customer. I approached them in a very polite manner and said, "I would like to pay for the treadmill and go home."

"We are taking care of this lady and you are going to have to wait," he replied.

"I was here first, and it does not take two of you to take care of one customer, and I would like one of you to take care of me." They continued to say I needed to wait until they finished.

While waiting, I began to get angry and finally I asked myself, "why am I angry?" The reason was that this situation reminded me of the beauty salon, and my time was not being respected. I said to my husband, "I feel like walking out and showing them you have to treat people with respect." My husband agreed and said he was thinking the same thing. I told him we have waited for over two hours and should speak with the manager. He answered, "It is up to you."

A man who claimed to be the store manager came to speak with us. He was obviously not the manager, so we left the store.

Again, I felt proud of myself, and understand today that I am valuable, and I deserve to be treated with respect. I used to be the person that stayed quiet and took the abuse. No more!

Because I followed my instincts by not allowing someone to step all over me, God talked to me though my instincts and I was able to get more than what I had expected. I realized what God was saying to me was, "Lillian, buy the things you need somewhere else." We did so, and ended up buying the big screen TV, and all the other items and saved a lot of money. [Thank you, Brands Mart!]

Setting Boundaries Enhances Integrity

I received a phone call from someone who was referred to me because she needed help in setting boundaries with her parents.

She told me her parents did not speak with her husband. Her husband had visited her parent's home on several occasions, and during those visits her parents ignored him. She went on to tell me that he decided not to visit them again unless he was treated with respect. Her parents did not approve of him, and they continued to treat her as if she was not married to him.

Her parents treated her to a 10-day cruise to Europe without including her husband.

My question to her was: "Why did you accept a trip that was only for you, if you are trying to have your husband included in everything? Moreover, according to you, the cruise is not until three months from now, and you could still cancel if you really wanted to set boundaries?"

She explained that her husband dislikes travel and the trip was already paid for.

I told her that if she decided to go on this trip, the message she was giving everyone, including her husband and herself, was that the trip was more important than the relationship with her husband.

She continued to justify her behavior, and I decided she was not really ready to set boundaries with her parents.

Because she really wanted to go on this trip, she was not willing to set the proper boundary, not realizing the high price she was paying by going on this cruise. She was compromising her integrity with herself. The result of taking this action was going to lower her self-esteem; it was going to damage her relationship with her husband, and more importantly, she was allowing her parents to continue to manipulate her.

In life, you are always paying a price. *There's no free lunch!*

You have to be aware of the price you might be paying in any situation. In this case, the price she was paying, by not setting the proper boundaries, was too high.

An Expensive Lesson

One day prior to my starting a seminar, my intuition was telling me to set boundaries with a friend of mine, and to tell him not to help me pick up any of my personal items, such as the boards that I use in the seminar. I did not listen to my intuition, because I did not want to hurt my friend's feelings. This friend of mine is not as careful with his valuables as I am with mine, and when I finished the seminar that day, he proceeded to put my boards away for me without my permission. The result was he broke one of my signs.

At first, I felt resentful toward him, but after a few minutes I realized the person I was really upset with was myself for not having set a boundary. It was my responsibility to tell him not to touch any of my personal items (personal space) without my permission or supervision.

That evening when I came home feeling upset, almost to the point of tears, I could not understand why. I stopped to analyze why I was feeling like that. Finally, I understood. It was my "inner child" that was upset because her toy was broken. Your "inner child" is the part inside you that never grows up. I realized I needed to talk to my inner child and explain to her that I would try to fix the board in the morning, or I would make a new one. As I was talking to my inner child, it occurred to me to take the sign back to the printer to see if he could fix it. As soon as that idea came to me the pain went away.

The very next morning, I went to the print shop, and he said he could fix it at a price of $75.00.

Not setting the proper boundary the night before, because of my people-pleasing attitude cost me $75.00 - what a lesson!

The lesson I discovered was three-fold. One, that my lack of action in making boundaries cost me $75.00 and pain. Second, that my inner child was involved in my seminars, and she felt the boards belonged to her, something I was not aware of. Today, I know the creative part of me is the child who is helping me to write this book, and more importantly, it is the creative force of the seminars. Third, now after this experience, under no condition do I place another person's feelings before mine. Taking care of Lillian is the absolute most important thing I have to do today without exception.

By taking care of yourself, you will be helping everyone around you become a better person. As your self-esteem improves, you help improve everyone else's self-esteem as well. People learn by what they see you do, not by what you tell them.

The Dog and the Alligator Story

If you take a dog that has never seen a horse before, and put him in a barnyard with a horse, at first he is afraid because of the horse's size and powerful movements. However, after a few minutes, the dog and the horse are running around the yard as the best of friends.

Take the same dog, assuming he has also never seen an alligator, and place him next to an alligator. The alligator does not move a muscle, stands less than a foot tall, and motionlessly, stares at the dog. Yet something tells the dog, "Don't go near the alligator!" If the Creator is so kind to the dog so as to give him this gift, would he be less kind to you? I think not!

Once you follow your inner guidance and trust yourself to set boundaries, you will be able to bring your guard down enough to allow yourself to establish intimate relationships. The dog can be close to the horse, but never to the alligator.

Closeness and Intimacy

We want closeness and intimacy. However, many of us lived in families where closeness and intimacy did not occur.

How can we know how to develop closeness and intimacy? By learning from those who have it.

CLOSENESS HAPPENS WHEN YOUR BOUNDARIES SOFTEN AND TOUCH SOMEONE ELSE'S BORDER.

INTIMACY HAPPENS WHEN YOUR BARRIER MERGES WITH SOMEONE ELSE'S.

Closeness feels good, and it is a comfortable, relaxed experience. On the other hand, intimacy is intense, and it can be:

1. Physical (sexual or non-sexual)
2. Emotional
3. Spiritual
    or a combination of any of the above.

Closeness is something we have control over. It has a lot to do with:

1. Being honest
2. Being open
3. Being there for the other person
4. Being compassionate
5. Being accepting of the other person

Security Instinct – Self-Preservation and Communication

6. Being concerned
7. Feeling safe

Closeness can be developed. On the other hand, the powerful connection of intimacy is a gift. It just happens.

Closeness May Lead You Into Intimacy

In order to experience closeness and intimacy both parties have to be ready. Sometimes we want to be close, or intimate, with someone who does not want the same. If we persist, the only thing we will achieve is frustration. This is where we can apply the phrase: "It takes two to tango."

The reason some people have problems with intimacy is because they are not connected with the emotional part of the security instinct - to be able to let others know how you feel, to express yourself, to feel affection, to be close, to be intimate, and to trust and confide. Trusting the other person being the most important factor of all. Intimacy is a way in which you communicate your true feelings.

To get close and intimate you have to be willing to give up control. You have to have trust in the other person, which is allowing yourself to be vulnerable without fear. You have to have a Self that is strong enough to allow closeness and intimacy, which will lead to happiness! Intimacy is one of life's most exhilarating feelings.

Intimacy and closeness will develop as you get in touch with your INSTINCTS. Allow yourself to experience them!

Remember, *Happiness Is An Inside Job!*

It is up to you!

Codependency

There are situations, which may hinder your happiness that you should avoid. Do not allow something like codependency rob you of your happiness. Codependency can keep you away from closeness and intimacy.

Who is a Codependent Person?

A codependent person is one who has allowed someone else's behavior to affect him or her, and is obsessed with controlling that person's behavior. The other person's action or behavior is their personal space, and it has to be respected even if we think the other person is wrong.

The process of growth from childhood is from dependent to independent to inter-dependent.

1. Dependent --------- When you are an infant or a child, you depend on your parents.

2. Independent ------ When you are free of the influence and control of others.

3. Inter-dependent --- Two or more healthy independent people sharing a mutual beneficial relationship without co-dependency.

In order to have a healthy intimate relationship you have to commit to:

1. Establish healthy boundaries all the time.

2. Allow yourself to get close and then intimate.

The problem some of us face is that we are afraid of commitment because of the possibility we might get hurt. It is better to try and be hurt than to never try at all!

Some people say, "I prefer my space and my freedom." What they are really saying might be, "I am afraid of commitment." Some people are as afraid to start a relationship, as they are afraid to finish one! They might be afraid to start a relationship because of fear of commitment, and they might be afraid to finish the relationship because of fear of change. I will discuss these fears in Chapter 7.

NON-PHYSICAL - time, talent, information and opportunity are another aspect of self-preservation.

So, What is Time?

Time is merely the order of events, not an entity in itself!

According to the dictionary, time is:

The sequential relations that any event has to another from past to present to future.

The basic element of time is an event. Everything is an event. Time is the occurrence of events in sequence, one after another. Controlling your time means controlling the events in your life.
You control your time; your time does not control you!

Every thing in life is a matter of belief. If you believe that you don't have enough time to do the things you want to do, then change your thinking and create time management.

Now, let's discuss time. How many times have you said to yourself, "When I have some time, I'm going to................."

Why don't you have the time today to do the things you want to do?

The answer is lack of time management!

Do you agree we all have 24-hours a day? Then, why are some people more productive than others in the same 24-hour day? Again, because of time management!

People, who say they do not have time, or are running out of time, fulfill their own prophecy! They end up with no time.

People with a sense of not enough time get stressed out and suffer from nervousness, high blood pressure, heart conditions, ulcers, fatigue, etc.

On the other hand, if you feel you have time to do everything you want to do, you will flow with life because God gave us all the same amount of time.

How about people who think they are going to have time in the future?

Have you ever said to yourself:
> I'll have time when the children go to college;
> I'll have time when I retire;
> I'll have time next month, next year, and that time never arrives!!

Every hour, since the beginning of time, has only had 60 minutes!

As you control the events in your life, you control your time!

Have you ever reacted to events and ended up doing whatever everybody else thought you ought to do, as opposed to what you thought you should do? How did that make you feel? Probably terrible! Right?

How do you feel inside when you are faced with events in your life you cannot control? Again, probably terrible! Right?

Do you have trouble being on time? Is this one of the values you have difficulty with?

If you do not respect your time because you do not respect yourself, would you respect someone else's time? Of course not!

Have you ever been late for an appointment? How many times have you blamed the traffic for being late?

The reality is, that most of the time you are late, it is because you leave late. The reason for this is you do not respect yourself enough to be on time.

What happens to your self-esteem when you cannot control your time?

It drops.

The 10 Minutes Late Story

A few years ago, I was supposed to meet a good friend at 8:00 a.m. for breakfast. The reason we were going to meet was because he was going to share his time to help me develop my business.

Follow Your Instincts

It was going to take me 30 minutes from my house to get to the restaurant. I left the house 10 minutes late, figuring the worst that could happen was I would be 10 minutes late. I arrived at the restaurant at 8:10 a.m. and could not find my friend. I described him to the waitress and asked her if she had seen him. She said a man matching the description was waiting for 20 minutes and had just left. I immediately called him on his cellular to get him to come back to the restaurant.

He said, "I waited 20 minutes for you."

I said, "Impossible, I was only 10 minutes late."

"No dear", he said. "You were 20 minutes late. I have a habit of getting to my appointments 10 minutes early. The reason for this is, that if I am not 10 minutes early, I consider myself already late. Call me and maybe we will set another appointment."

The result, I drove for 30 minutes to an appointment I was not able to keep, and the real reason was because I left the house 10 minutes late.

After the above incident happened to me, I got into the habit of being 10 minutes early for all my appointments. This new attitude has done wonders for me. If I am going to be in an area that might have too much traffic, I might leave 30 minutes early so that I can be 10 minutes early.

I changed from a person that you could guarantee would be late to a very punctual person. It is a great feeling to know people think of me as a punctual person today. When people say to me, "You are punctual," I feel my self-esteem rising. The silent message people are telling me is, "We know you respect yourself and your time. You are a person of integrity." This message makes me feel good about myself!

Every time you do something to feel good about yourself, you increase your self-esteem.

My suggestion to you is get into a habit of saying to yourself:

> IF I AM NOT 10 MINUTES EARLY,
> I AM ALREADY LATE!

Start by respecting other people's time, and soon you will be respecting your own; or vice versa, start respecting your time, and soon you will be respecting other people's time.

What Can You Control?

1. The time you get up.
2. What you wear.
3. How early are you going to leave your home to get to work on time.
4. What you eat.
5. Who you eat with.
6. How you react to somebody else's attitude.
7. What you are doing this evening, etc.

All of these events focus on you! You do these things. You control these events.

The only thing you have total control over is you!

The more you manage you and the things you do, the better you are going to feel about yourself and the better self-esteem you will have. Time, the controlling of the sequence of events in your life, is part of your security instinct, and it is connected to your self-esteem, your social instinct. This is the explanation of why, when you accomplish everything you set out to do in a workday, you feel good about yourself. When you allow people to interrupt your day, you are allowing them to rearrange your planned sequence of events. So, never say your time is not important, and do not allow anyone else to tell you that either.

What will be the result of your controlling the events in your life?

The result will be that you will feel confident, powerful and happy. All of these feelings will provide better self-esteem. With the control of the events in your life, you will achieve inner peace.

What is inner peace?

Inner peace is having serenity, balance, and harmony through the control of events, and this is achieved through event/time management.

Time Management

The objective of time management is inner peace!

Instead of thinking time management, think event management. Get into the habit of thinking of what events you can and cannot control. Concentrate only on the events you can control. Embrace the "now" and what you can do now.

There are events you can't control. Trying to control and manipulate situations or events outside of yourself, or the behaviors and lives of others, such as your spouse, children, employees, co-workers, etc. will drain your energies. You end up wasting a lot of time. *Stop wasting time and focus on what you can do.*

There are some events you really can control, but mentally and emotionally you believe you cannot.

If you believe you can, you are right.
If you believe you cannot, you are also right!

Which belief are you going to choose for yourself?

There is a direct relationship between self-esteem and productive work.

The better you feel about yourself, the more productive you are; the more productive you are, the better you feel about yourself.

EVENT CONTROL

SELF-ESTEEM  PRODUCTIVITY

If your self-esteem drops, what happens to your productivity? Of course, it drops as well.

Follow Your Instincts

When your productivity drops, so does your event control!

High self-esteem creates event control, event control creates productivity, and productivity creates better self-esteem.

As you improve your self-esteem, you feel better about yourself. As you feel better about yourself, you will be more productive in whatever you do.

The importance of becoming more productive is that as productivity increases you will take less time to accomplish goals, and consequently, you will have more time for the activities you value. In turn, you will increase your sense of self-worth and your self-esteem.

As you get more control over events, you will feel better about yourself and will end up with better self-esteem.

Suppose I say to you:

Today I am giving you twenty four thousand dollars in cash (one thousand for every hour). However, there is a condition: you must spend it in one day. If there is any money left, you cannot keep it or save it for another day. What would you do? Would you be careful with every thousand dollars, and make sure you spend them properly? I imagine you would! Why don't you do the same thing with time!

You have twenty-four hours every day no more, no less. You cannot save any time to spend it another day. -- *Time wasted is time lost forever!*

Time is just like money --- It is a precious commodity. use it wisely!

When you decide to spend time on something, you have decided not to spend it on something else. Be wise how you choose to spend your time.

Goal Setting

How can you use your time correctly?

The answer is goal setting!

The first thing about setting goals is that you have to know what you want! For right now let's say this book has magic! Whatever you want will be manifested at this time.

What do you want?

Why don't you have it in your life already?

You don't have it in your life already because of your beliefs. You have to increase belief in yourself to achieve what you want.
Goals have to be yours! They cannot be what someone else wants for you.
If you do not set goals, you just exist, you are not living, or at least not to the degree you could be if you took charge.

If you fail to plan, you plan to fail!

Many times the reason we do not set goals is to avoid responsibility! Is that your case?

Follow Your Instincts

Only you can honestly answer this question. Begin to set goals, and your life will take on a new meaning.

Once you make a decision to create goals, then, you can follow these suggestions:

Goals must be:

1. IN WRITING - An unwritten goal is merely a wish. Writing them forces you to be specific and realistic.

2. SPECIFIC --The goal cannot be vague such as: I want to make a lot of money. Your goal should be expressed as the future being in the present, such as: I make $50,000 a year (as though it has already been achieved).

3. STATED IN THE POSITIVE --- Notice how in the above example it is stated positively and in the present tense.

4. HAVE A STEP-BY-STEP PLAN OF ACTION

5. DATED   It is now on or before (date)_____ and I have in my possession (goal)_____ if it is in Divine order.

6. VISUALIZE REACHING YOUR GOALS ---- Use the power of affirmations.

Security Instinct – Self-Preservation and Communication

What is the first thing people do when they are going to get married? Of course, they set a DATE. After you have a date set, then, everything has to occur before that time for the wedding to occur. It is the same with goal setting. The first thing you have to do is to have a date! Then you have to outline the step-by-step plan of action that has to occur before the deadline.

Goals force you to plan. -- I will have a plan. I might not follow it exactly, but I will have it.

Do you know what the ten most powerful words in the world are?

IF IT'S GOING TO BE, IT IS UP TO ME

If it is going to be, it is up to you. Only you can plan your life. Only you can set your own goals, and only you can achieve your goals! Only you can bring yourself happiness!

There are seven areas in your life in which you should set goals, and these are:

1. Personal Development
   a. Physical
   b. Emotional
   c. Spiritual

2. Marriage and Family

3. Financial

4. Professional

5. Social and Friends

6. Service

7. Play and Pleasure---- Have fun! ---- Many people do not plan fun events.

Many times we do not set goals because of fear of change, fear of failure, or fear of success. I will discuss these fears in Chapter 7.

Once you have a goal, what is the worst enemy you have to fight?

Procrastination

The most common reason you procrastinate is because a certain task is unpleasant to you, or perhaps, because you have to get out of your comfort zone.

Setting and reaching goals means doing something new, leaving your familiar territory, getting out of your comfort zone, and exploring new frontiers!!

Procrastination will keep you away from reaching your goals.

The reasons we procrastinate are:

1. Unclear goals
2. Over-committing
3. Lack of information
4. Fear of failure

5. Fear of success
6. Fear of change
7. General disorganization

Procrastination is a deadly time robber and a terrible enemy.

Tomorrow is the best labor saving device ever invented.

If your goal is something you intensely desire, develop an urgency about it. Do not act as if you have a thousand years to live! Go ahead and fire your worst enemy, procrastination!

A great vehicle you can use to avoid procrastination is to say to yourself:

I AM A DO IT NOW PERSON

Three suggestions for overcoming procrastination:

1. Set a deadline - Setting a deadline allows you to be realistic.

2. Do the most unpleasant part first -- Then you can look forward to the more enjoyable task later

3. Build in a Reward -- Treat yourself to something nice every time you reach a goal. For example, go to dinner, buy yourself something you always wanted, go on a trip, etc.

Follow Your Instincts

Another reason you procrastinate is because some tasks seem overwhelming to you. To avoid getting overwhelmed, take a goal and divide as follows:

1. Long term
2. Intermediate
3. Weekly or daily

For example: If you need to lose 30 pounds
Goal = 30 pounds lost by _____
(write future date, i.e., four months from now)

1. LONG TERM = Goal = 30 pounds in a four month period.

2. INTERMIDIATE = Divide the goal into 4 month or 8 pounds a month.

3. WEEKLY = Divide the monthly goal into four weeks. Lose 2 pounds a week.

If a task is too big, divide the goal into smaller steps, and then, take baby steps in the direction of your goal.

If setting a goal is so easy, what is stopping you from getting what you want? Fear, self doubt, but primarily, your self-talk!

According to psychologists, we think between 40 to 50 thousand thoughts a day, and 87% of those thoughts are negative because we live in a negative world.

Security Instinct – Self-Preservation and Communication

When you are looking at what you want, you have to be very careful that you do not give *negative messages* to yourself *thereby talking yourself out of your goal!*
You have to start controlling what you tell yourself. Make sure the messages you tell yourself are positive. For example:

I know I can do it, I believe in me.

THESE ARE THE MESSAGES YOU SHOULD BE TELLING YOURSELF ALL THE TIME.

When the message is negative, stop your inner dialog by saying to yourself "cancel, cancel," and change it to a positive message.

Suppose you say to yourself, "I do not think I can lose 30 pounds in 4 months." You need to say to yourself, "Cancel, cancel," and then say the new affirmation in a positive manner. "I can lose 30 pounds in 4 months; I know I can do it!"

No goal setting is going to help you if you do not believe in yourself.

START BELIEVING IN YOU!

Once you have established a goal, one thing is certain: you are going to have some opposition not only from your own inner dialogue, but also from people in your life. Do not allow negative messages from others to affect your thinking process.

Follow Your Instincts

Example:
Someone says to you, "Be real, you tried dieting before! Be happy with the extra weight. Accept yourself as you are."---- *Baloney!*

Say to yourself, "Cancel, cancel, I can do it! This goal is the perfect one for me, because it is my goal!"

When you have a goal, and try to convince others of it, they might tell you your goal is not good, and that it has no value, and this might cause you to doubt your goal and your ability to achieve it.

Do not listen to anyone, including your negative Self. Follow your dream!

Talent ---- You are born with the ability (talent), with practice it becomes a skill. Talents, no matter how small, with practice will improve your self-esteem and allow you to become a more accomplished person.

Information ----- The more information you have about yourself, your immediate surroundings, and your world in general, the greater your chances for your survival.

Opportunity ------ Opportunities knock all the time as gifts from the Universe. Having the capacity to recognize them by the usage of information and talent will lead you to capture these opportunities, and will enhance your chances of self-preservation.

Time, talent, information, and opportunity will result in you having increased security. Self-preservation is man's strongest instinct.

12 Steps Towards Building a Positive Mental Attitude

1. With the power of affirmation, condition your mind at the beginning of each day.
2. Start each day by being grateful for the good and the bad (the bad being an opportunity to grow).
3. Concentrate on what you can do and do it now!
4. Change unpleasant circumstances with immediate action.
5. Refuse to permit yourself to worry and turn this wasted energy into action.
6. Look at your life as a continuous learning process, and learn from each experience.
7. Be open-minded.
8. Go out of your way to appreciate other people's good qualities.
9. Be patient and generous with others. Don't place expectations on others. People will do what they choose to do.
10. Accept criticism as an opportunity for self-examination.
11. Keep your mind "goal focused."
12. Get a mentor in your life.

Whatever you think and believe you can do,
you accomplish!

2. COMUNICATION

Communicating is the most important thing we do every day!
 In life, being a good communicator will take you to the top of anything you do!

Follow Your Instincts

Do you think you are a public speaker? If not, what are you? A private speaker? That means you speak in the privacy of your home, perhaps only in the privacy of your bedroom?

We are all public speakers! We are always speaking in public to people everywhere we go, but this does not mean we are communicating.

To communicate is part of the instinct. Language is a skill.

The cave man did not have language, as we know it today; however, they communicated, because it was part of their God-given instinct.

My husband has two employees, one that does not speak English; the other does not speak Spanish. However, they communicate by sign language, and what is funny is they like working with each other.

Sign language is another skill that can be used to communicate.

TO COMMUNICATE IS:

1. To make known
2. To pass information
3. To convey information
4. To transfer or to transmit and receive information

COMMUNICATION IS SAYING
THE RIGHT THING
TO THE RIGHT PERSON
IN THE RIGHT PLACE
AT THE RIGHT TIME

Security Instinct – Self-Preservation and Communication

You are born with the ability (part of the instinct) to communicate. With practice the ability becomes a skill!

Learning to be a good communicator takes time and commitment. You can do it!

When you are trying to express yourself, do not assume the other person understands you. Learn to express your needs (instinct) and wants (desire) as if the other person does not have a clue as to what you are trying to say.

Listening

A very important part of communication is to listen. How many times have you felt you were not listened to?

More importantly, how many times have you not paid attention when someone was speaking to you?

If you want people to listen to you, you have to start by listening to them!

To be a good communicator, you have to become a good listener! Become an active listener. Listening is hearing and understanding what someone is saying to you.

Listening is an essential part of successful living.

When you listen, you can learn. The reason you learn is because you expose yourself to new information, and you can also gain insight into the thoughts, feelings, and needs of other people. The only real way to connect with others is through listening.

Listening is much more than hearing!

You hear an ambulance when you are driving; you hear

music in the background in the car, in a restaurant, and in the office. Hearing is the automatic reaction of your ears to sound. *Listening takes effort, thought, and concentration.*

You listen for the door bell when you are expecting company; you listen for the telephone to ring when you are expecting an important call; you listen to the words when your significant other tells you he or she loves you.

To be a better communicator what you have to achieve is perceptive listening.

Perceptive listening is hearing more than words. It is listening to the other person's opinions, emotions, and feelings. It is listening to the precise meaning of the words or sounds presented. It is listening to what the person is really saying.

You have the ability to listen on several levels:

1. Listen for information --- When you ask for direction.
2. Listen for opinions ---- A person's choice of words and tone of voice will reveal an opinion.
3. Listen for feeling ------- If you pay close attention to what someone is saying you can discover the feeling behind those words.

The "I Message"

When you have to respond to statements or actions of others, the best method to not offend the other person is to use what I call the "I Message".

The "I Message" goes like this:

When you do _____ to me, "I" feel _____.

The reason why it is so important to be in touch with your instinct is because once you are clear about what your needs are, then you will be able to set boundaries or clearly express your opinions with the "I" message without offending others.

What happens when you get upset is you begin to tell others the things that are wrong with them, instead of using the "I" message! – True or Not?

The Feel-Felt-Found Method

You could also use the FEEL ---- FELT ---- FOUND method.

It goes like this. When you are talking to someone and they are upset, you say, "I know how you feel (of course, only if it is true). However, I feel (or felt)_____, and what I found was _____.

SUMMARY

Security instinct has to do with self-preservation by seeking food, shelter, clothing and personal space. It is also your ability to communicate with others. The security instinct is composed of two parts: self-preservation and communication.

1. Self-Preservation

Self-preservation pertains to physical well being.

> a. PHYSICAL - food, shelter, clothing, health aids, money as a medium of exchange, and personal space, which is the area where you end and the other person begins. We have personal space in the areas of physical, emotional, and spiritual.

Being in touch with your personal space and setting boundaries will help you build a healthy self-esteem, and you will feel better about yourself, and you can achieve closeness and intimacy.

> b. NON-PHYSICAL - time, talent, information and opportunity, are another aspect of self-preservation.

Time ---- Time is the occurrence of events in sequence, one after another. Then, controlling your time, means controlling the events in your life.

Talent --- You are born with an ability (talent). With practice, it becomes a skill. Talents, no matter how small, with practice will improve your self-esteem and allow you to become a more accomplished person.

Information ----- The more information you have about yourself, immediate surroundings, and your world in general, the greater your chances for your survival.

Opportunity ------ Opportunities knock all the time as gifts from the universe. Having the capacity to recognize them by the usage of information and talent, will lead you to capture these opportunities, enhancing your chances of self- preservation.

Time, talent, information and opportunity will result in you having increased security. Self-preservation is man's strongest instinct.

2. Communication

Communicating is the most important thing we do every day!

In life, being a good communicator will take you to the top of anything you do!

COMMUNICATION IS SAYING
THE RIGHT THING
TO THE RIGHT PERSON
IN THE RIGHT PLACE
AT THE RIGHT TIME

Your communication skills can improve by active listening to what others really have to say and by accepting others opinions and feelings.

Follow Your Instincts

The security instinct has to do with self-preservation and communication. Being in touch with this instinct will assist you in achieving security.

Embrace life and use your God-given security instinct to achieve what you want in your life.

Remember, you are the best gift the Creator gave you. You deserve the best!

Chapter 4

SEX INSTINCT -- SEXUAL IDENTITY AND SEXUAL RELATIONS

What is Sexual Instinct?

Sexual instinct is your sexual identity and your sexual relations.

Sexual issues have been a taboo subject and not talked about for generations because of the belief that they are dirty! If this is the case, why did God make it part of our instincts? Because it is natural!

Sex instinct, your sense of male or female, and everything involved with your sexual interaction, is composed of two parts: sexual identity and sexual relations.

1. Sexual Identity

Sexual Identity is your sense of yourself as male or female, your sense of being maternal or paternal, feeling attractive or attracted, and feeling stimulating or stimulated.

Your sexual identity is your connection to your sexuality. It is understanding that you have male and female hormones, and for that reason you have male as well as female qualities within you. One becomes more dominant than the other, making you a male or a female. There are, however, circumstances of male/female imbalance that produce mixed gender characteristics.

In the Tao philosophy

Yin is the female principle or energy representing the force of the earth.

Yang is the masculine principle representing the spirit.

Personal power results from a balance of masculine and feminine energies.

Aggressive energy is masculine and passive energy is feminine. Personal power is the result of balancing these two energies.

When I was growing up I always heard that boys were better than girls, so I decided to develop some male characteristics to compete with boys. I became aggressive; I used my aggressiveness in business and became successful. As a child, I played boy games to become very competitive, and it was not until a few years ago that I truly became aware of my feminine side.

Your sexual identity will manifest itself in many areas of your life, at home, at work, in social gatherings, and in everything you do.

Certain roles have been attached to male and others to female, for example: The male was the provider and went to work, and the female stayed home raising the family. If you are a female and have a male mentality, like me, you are going to prefer to go out and work rather than take care of house chores.

Dressing is a way you convey sexual identity. The clothes you wear convey a message of how you feel inside about your sexuality. People who are not truly connected to their sexuality tend not to dress attractively, because they are hiding their sexuality.

Think attractive and you will dress attractively!

You may not want to dress in a sexy manner for fear that you may be attractive and attract the opposite sex. Dressing may be a form of flirting. In my case, I dressed very sexy at work to compensate for my male mentality. Of course, I did this at a subconscious level. I was not aware that I was doing so until I got in touch with my sexuality. I was dressing attractively, but not in order to flirt.

Sex and sexuality issues were some of the things that were not discussed when we were growing up. As a matter of fact, when we began to discover our sexual identity as teenagers, many of our parents made us feel guilty or dirty about this thing that is so natural and part of our instincts.

It was not until recently that woman's sexuality has been addressed. Up to now, women did not find it normal to enjoy sex. There is a new recognition that female sexuality is important! For that matter, sexuality is as important to females as it is to males!

You have to claim God's gift to you! Your sexual identity is part of your sex instinct. That is what God wants for you. *At least I know that God wants it for me!*

Being Maternal or Paternal is Part of the Sexual Identity and Thus part of Your Sex Instinct

The maternal/paternal instinct is one of the strongest of all of the instincts.

One of my objectives with this section of the book is to help you get in touch with you maternal/paternal instinct.

Grandma's Story

There is a true story of a grandmother whose grandchild was trapped beneath a car and the grandmother used extraordinary energy to lift the car. Two men that were standing there could not do it. The explanation is that her maternal instinct allowed her to use extraordinary force. If she did not move the car, her grandchild would have died.

The Gorilla Story

Another story is that of the child that fell into the female Gorilla's territory at the zoo. The people watching the incident at the time were concerned for the child's safety. However, what they saw was amazing. The female Gorilla, using her maternal instinct, knew the child needed help and held the child in her arms and caressed him until help arrived. The female gorilla's action was a big surprise to everyone watching.

The Neighborhood Cat Story

A neighborhood cat began to visit my back patio. Feeling sorry for the cat I began to feed him. At the beginning, the cat was afraid to let me get close to him. I slowly began to gain his trust by putting food out for him and then walking away. Every time, I would get closer and closer, until one day he allowed me to touch him, but very little. He did not feel comfortable with my getting too close. In the early morning, all I would have to say is "come kitty," and he would immediately come. Then, he went and brought me two more friends.

Several months passed and still "Calico" (that is what I named him) would not allow me to get too close. One day, I noticed Calico was getting too fat on the same amount of food that I was feeding him. I realized Calico was a pregnant female, and I changed her name to Calica.

One day Calica did not come for her morning food, and I realized she must have had kittens. Since I have a big German Shepherd, I figured she did not feel safe having them in my backyard. I went through the neighborhood looking for Calica to no avail. I was worried about her not having food.

Two weeks later my next-door neighbor called me to tell me Calica was in his patio with one kitten. Then, we discovered three more. I immediately took food to her, and she seemed so pleased to see me. The very next morning, Calica was at her usual place on my patio, waiting for her food, while her kittens were safe on my neighbor's patio.

From the instinct's point of view, her maternal instinct told her to keep her kittens away from my dog, and at the same time, her instinct of self-preservation (security instinct) told her to come back because she needed to take care of herself in order to care of her kittens.

When Calica came back, she allowed me for the first time to caress her for almost one hour. She was giving nurturing (maternal instinct) to her kittens, and she need to replenish her own supply.

Between my neighbor and I, we built a bed for Calica and her four kittens. A lot of people began to come over to see them, and one morning when I went to see Calica, she had taken the four kittens to a more secure place. I did not blame her, as she sensed some people were ready to take them. Calica, at an instinctual level, sensed she was going to lose her litter, and her maternal instinct went into action, and she protected them by moving them to a safer place.

My Dog Champ

Another example is my three-year-old trained dog that I purchased to protect me. His name is Champ. The day I picked him up, the trainer said it would take the dog about three weeks to get attached to me. I did not accept what the trainer said, and I began to talk to Champ's instincts. I said things like:

> This is going to be your new home.
> I am going to take care of you.
> I am going to feed you and bathe you.
> I love you.
> I will always take care of you, all your needs will be met.
> I am going to play with you.
> You are a nice dog.
> We are going to be the best of friends.

When I went back the following week to the trainer for the protection lessons, the trainer was shocked at how bonded Champ and I had become. To me it was not a surprise, I knew, that even though Champ did not understand the words I was saying to him, at an instinctual level, he did understand the feelings behind those words.

When we are connected with our instincts, God communicates with us through intuition. Champ intuitively knew what I was saying.

The Baby Bird Story

One day my husband and I were driving home, and we found a baby bird in the middle of the street. My natural nurturing instinct made me get out of the car and take the baby bird off the road. I noticed the mother was nearby calling it, but she was allowing the bird to come back to her on its own, so that the baby bird could learn and grow.

What I learned was that the natural instinct of the mother bird was to protect the young bird, but at the same time allow the process of learning to occur. Humans, on the other hand, many times do too much for their children, not allowing them space for growth.

You can use the maternal/paternal instinct to influence people in your life, especially your children, and most importantly you can help the child that lives inside you. For that matter, you can help anyone you come in contact with.

Messages Given to Children

There are only two kinds of messages you can give your children, positive or negative.

Negative messages become hurtful ones that diminish

your child's self-worth and self-esteem.

Loving, positive messages reinforce your child's self-image, helping to raise their self-esteem.

Your messages become your children's truth and that truth becomes their self-esteem. Their self-esteem becomes their life!

Pay attention to the messages you give your children. More importantly, pay attention to the messages you give your inner child. The importance of this is that you will treat others as you treat yourself. Begin to treat yourself with love.

Parenting Should be From the Heart

Five tools for parenting from the heart

1. Praise --- This is one of the best ways to improve your children's self-esteem. Give empowering messages. Whenever you see your children being good, acknowledge them, even for the smallest actions.

2. Listen --- How many times do you wish you would have been listened to? Do not make the same mistake with your children. Make them feel important by listening to what they have to say.

3. Teach --- Give of your time and share what you have learned. Use the power of asking questions to assist your children in arriving at their own conclusions.

4. Model --- Be an example. Children learn from copying or imitating what their parents do.

5. Love --- Love your children unconditionally.

Praise

Praising your child is one of the most important things you can do for their self-esteem.

Your children's self-esteem is apparent in everything they do. Make sure you are giving the right encouragement and praise.

Give messages like:

1. You can do it.
2. I know you can do it.
3. I believe in you.
4. You can do anything you set your mind to.
5. I have all the faith in the world in you.
6. You are important and your decisions count.

When you give loving messages, you are boosting your child's self-worth, and raising your child's self-esteem. Consequently, you will help shape their lives.

If the child inside you (your inner child) received negative messages when you were growing up; this information will assist you in healing yourself. As you learn to praise, listen, and teach your inner child, you will be healing the inner child, and helping your self-esteem improve.

In order to be able to give loving messages to your children, you must first give loving, positive messages to yourself. You can't give away what you do not have!

Listen

Listening is another way to help improve your child's self-esteem. What children need the most is to be listened to. Help your child to feel good with whatever he or she has to say, even if you do not agree.

What kind of message are you giving your children, if you always have something better to say?

The message you would be giving your children is that their ideas and opinions do not count. This is a rapid way to lower your child's self-esteem.
The child may end up saying to themselves, "What is the point, no matter how creative I become, my parents are always better." This will also shoot down your child's creativity.
When you listen, it is important that you pay attention to your child's feelings and validate them. It does not matter if you think your child should not be feeling that way!

How many times when you were a child were you told, "You should not feel that way."?

Did that make you feel any better? The answer is: No.

All you wanted was to be acknowledged for what you were feeling, irrespective of whether it was right or wrong.

Sex Instinct – Sexual Identity and Sexual Relations

Feelings are just feelings, they are not right or wrong! They are just feelings.

Do not make the same mistake with your children. Acknowledge them with the power of listening. Accept your child's feelings without judgment. Denying feelings creates dysfunctional families.

A child whose feelings are not acknowledged cannot grow up whole!

When children do not connect with their feelings, they become fragmented and lose their sense of wholeness. This is the time when children become disconnected from their instincts.

What you must do is assist your child with the behavior that follows a feeling.

As a parent, listening assists your child to connect with his/her instinct.

Use the thought → feeling → action process, so that you can listen to what your child is really saying.

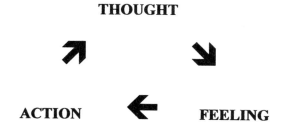

Follow Your Instincts

When you listen you:

1. Validate your child's feelings, helping to enhance your child's self-esteem.

2. You acknowledge they have something important to say, and that you value their opinion, allowing the development of their self-worth.

3. When you listen to their solutions to their problems, you help develop their problem-solving skills.

4. By asking questions and listening, you expand your child's creativity.

Teach

Teach your children to focus on their strengths rather than their weaknesses. By doing this you help improve your child's self-worth, and consequently, their self-esteem will rise.

When you are teaching, use the method of asking questions instead of telling them what you think. Help them find their own conclusions, help them develop their creativity, talents, and abilities that otherwise might never be discovered.

The objective of asking questions is to assist your child in presenting information in an orderly manner.

Ask questions like:

1. What do you think?

Sex Instinct – Sexual Identity and Sexual Relations

2. What are you feeling?
3. Could you have done that differently?
4. What can you learn from that?
5. What is the value you have learned from that experience?
6. How do you think you are going to feel if you do that?
7. How do you think _____ is going to feel if you do that?
8. What do you think will happen if you do that?
9. Are those the results you want for yourself?
10. What do you want to happen?
11. Who else is going to benefit if you do that?
12. In what other way could you solve this problem?
13. What do you think you should do?
14. What have you done today that can help you feel good about yourself?

This last question helps tremendously in improving your child's self-esteem.

By asking questions you assist them to think for themselves.

So, ASK QUESTIONS, ASK QUESTIONS, ASK QUESTIONS.

When you ask questions, you are acknowledging your child as a thinking individual and that their opinions count.

There is a proverb that says:

TELL ME AND I WILL FORGET;
SHOW ME AND I MAY REMEMBER;
INVOLVE ME AND I WILL UNDERSTAND!

By asking questions, you involve them.

An Important Part of Teaching Includes Discipline

According to the dictionary, discipline is:

1. Training to act in accordance with rules.
2. Instructions and exercises designed to train proper conduct or action.
3. Behaving in accordance with rules of conduct.
4. Establishing a set of rules and regulations.
5. Re-educating by way of correction and training.

Have you ever felt guilty after you disciplined your child, or have you ever not disciplined your child for fear of being a bad parent?

If you knew you were only helping your child to behave in accordance with rules and regulations, you will not have feel guilty.

The reason a lot of teenagers have problems is because they were not disciplined at the right age.

Animals, as part of their maternal/paternal instinct, discipline their young.

We adopted a female Rottweiler dog. Then, about three weeks later, we adopted a younger male Rottweiler. The female took the role of mother, and when the young male did something wrong, she gently bit his leg to let him know his behavior was wrong. The female dog was applying discipline as part of her maternal instinct. She was showing the rules to the young male. After she applied the punishment, she would lick the young dog as if she was saying, "I love you, and all I am doing is helping you be better."

Discipline helps maintain the limits of behavior you have created for your family.

Model

Most importantly, remember children learn by imitating adults. Be an example. You cannot give your children messages you are not willing to practice yourself.

When you display your healthy self-esteem, your child sees that your life is fulfilling. Your child sees the power you have to manifest choices in your life and will copy that. On the other hand, if you suffer from low self-esteem you will reflect that, and that is exactly what your child will copy.

Were you raised by a parent that had high self-esteem, but you ended up with low self-esteem? Probably not.

High self-esteem parents raise ---- high self-esteem children

and

Low self-esteem parents raise ---- low self-esteem children

Follow Your Instincts

The best gift you can give your children is to work on you. Improve your self-esteem in order to be a good role model!

Love

Love your children unconditionally, even if they have traits you do not like. Unconditional love is to not withhold love for any reason whatsoever. Place conditions only on behavior, not on your love.

Remember the car example from the social instinct chapter? Suppose you have a car that needs a new battery, a new alternator, or some new tires. Does this mean the car is not good, or does it mean it has areas that need fixing?

With children it is the same thing. They might have areas that need fixing. This does not make them defective. With love, you can empower them to change whatever it is that might need changing.

It is very important to understand that if you have a defect (an area that needs change), it does not make you defective. What it means is you have an area you have to work on.

It is also true that if you make a mistake, it does not mean you are a mistake!

Love your children as well as your inner child, unconditionally, with the good and the bad! Most importantly, love your children while they are trying to change.

In loving your children, use hugging, touching, and kissing.

We need:

> 4 Hugs for Survival
> 8 Hugs for Maintenance
> 12 Hugs for Growth

My question is: "Have you hugged your child today?"

The biggest message you can get from this book:

LOVE YOUR CHILDREN UNCONDITIONALLY!

Parents as Leaders

Being a parent is being a leader. Whether in business or at home, a leader motivates and empowers people to work and do things based on their own ideas and their own internal commitment.

Your job as a parent is to lead your child through life. The best way to accomplish this is by being an example. Remember, children learn by imitating.

Your children (including your inner child) will flourish beyond your fondest dreams, when you provide the support and help they need to be the best they can be.

TREAT YOUR CHILDREN NOT AS THEY ARE TODAY, BUT AS YOU KNOW THEY CAN BE TOMORROW!

The Farmer's Principle

Do you know about the Farmer's Principle?

This principle is that the farmer has to:

1. Prepare the land.
2. Plant the seed.
3. Water and fertilize (in some circumstances every day).
4. Have patience to finally harvest a good crop.

The farmer cannot skip any of these steps, or take any shortcuts, if he is to harvest a good crop!

Raising children is pretty much like the farmer's principle. If you want healthy children, you have to put in the time and energy required everyday!

Many parents complain about their children; however, the first thing they should look at is if they are devoting the necessary time required to raise them properly.

The Pinching Theory

There is a gardener's practice that is called pinching!

Pinching in gardening is eliminating the dried out flowers of a plant. The theory is the dried out flowers rob the plant's energy.

You have to use the pinching principle when working with the inner child. This child may have some painful experiences from childhood. You have to treat these painful experiences as dried flowers robbing its energy. You must remove these harmful areas from your tree. The tree of life that is your inner child!

Eliminate the negative areas of your inner child, so that beautiful positive energy can take their place!

Sex Instinct – Sexual Identity and Sexual Relations

Remember the bamboo tree example? Well, here it is again! Raising children is like growing a bamboo tree. It takes time, love, and energy, and you cannot skip any steps!

The School Teacher Story

A friend of mine, a schoolteacher, called me one evening just after meeting with the parents of a student that was facing the possibility of not graduating from high school. To her surprise, when she met with the parents to tell them what was happening, the parents became very upset and verbally abusive, including accusing her of being an incompetent teacher.

My friend was so upset, she called me to help her find out what was going on with her feelings. I explained the parents were reacting from the parental part of the sex instinct. They felt if their child did not graduate, it would mean they failed as parents. Therefore, it was better to blame someone else than look inside themselves.

I also asked her, "Have you honestly done everything possible to help this student?"

"Yes," she said. She had even helped after hours.

"You are upset because you think your social instinct is not satisfied," I explained. "Your pride, which is satisfaction in one's work or achievement, was affected. Your prestige, which is, recognition, feeling valuable, important, and respected was also affected. In addition, since the parents said you were not a competent teacher, your security instinct was also affected, as it threatened your livelihood, by questioning your knowledge, skills, and abilities. If you did everything you could to help the student, then it is simply a matter of what they think, and you are powerless over that."

Once my friend understood the parents were reacting to their own feelings of fear, which had nothing to do with her, and that perhaps they were not satisfying their sex instinct, as they were feeling they were not being good parents, she was able to eliminate her defensiveness. Armed with this awareness, my friend called the parents and explained their son's behavior was not a reflection of their parental capabilities. The parents then became cooperative, helping the child to finally graduate.

This is the reason why understanding instincts is so important. It does not matter what we might be facing in life. We can understand not only what is troubling us, but also what is troubling the other person. This makes it possible for us to be happier and help make other people's lives happier as well.

Gifts to Give to Your Children

Give your children a proper attitude that will prepare them for life. This attitude is achieved by instilling in them the following gifts of values and principles:

1. Honesty
2. Responsibility
3. Integrity
4. Compassion
5. Balance
6. Humor

The best way to pass these values/principles to your children is by example. Live these values and your children will copy.

1. The Gift of Honesty

According to the dictionary, Honesty is:

Truthfulness, sincerity, frankness, uprightness and freedom from deceit or fraud.

When your child is dishonest and has the courage to let you know, praise the fact he or she had the courage to be honest.

Your children need to know they can trust you with their secrets. In order for them to trust you, you must start by trusting them.

2. The Gift of Responsibility

According to the dictionary, Responsibility is:

1. Being responsible, reliable, dependable, answerable and accountable.
2. Having the capacity for moral decision and therefore being accountable.
3. Being able to discharge obligations and pay debts.

Responsibility is the ability to respond properly to events in your life.

When you give your children the gift of responsibility, you are helping them take charge of their lives.

It is a good idea to teach financial responsibility from a very young age, letting them know they have to pay their debts.

3. The Gift of Integrity

According to the dictionary, Integrity is:

Adherence to moral and ethical principles; soundness of moral character, and the continuous practice of honesty.

When you practice continuous honesty, you acquire integrity. Achieving integrity is the best way to improve your self-esteem.

When your children do not have integrity, they end up feeling like victims. They give their power away, and are always blaming someone else for the circumstances in their lives.

Integrity is being continuously honest, whether you are being watched or not. Integrity creates trust and is very important in creating healthy relationships.

4. The Gift of Compassion

According to the dictionary, Compassion is:

A feeling of deep sympathy for another's suffering or misfortune, accompanied by a desire to help alleviate the pain. Tenderness, coming from the heart.

Being compassionate comes from a special place in your

heart and mind. It is appreciating everyone, especially yourself. It means acknowledging yourself for what you are doing and becoming.

Compassion to me means walking in the other person's shoes, accepting their opinions and feelings, even if they are different than mine.

When you show your children compassion, they will usually show compassion for others!

5. The Gift of Balance

According to the dictionary, Balance is:

The state of equilibrium.
A state of stability as of the body or emotions.
A state of harmony.
The act of creating a state of balance.
Equality between the two sides.

Balance is necessary in everything in life!

Help your children create balance between going to school, doing homework, playtime, TV, rest, fun, etc.

It is important to create a sense of balance in your children's life by having balance in your own.

6. The Gift of Humor

According to the dictionary, Humor is:

The faculty of perceiving, appreciating, or expressing

what is amusing or comical.
A temporary mood or frame of mind.
It is frequently used to illustrate some fundamental absurdity in human nature or conduct.

When you have a sense of humor, you display joy and trust the process of life.
Teasing, sometimes mistakenly used as humor, hurts and can diminish your child's fragile self-esteem.
Kidding, on the other hand, can often be quite humorous when used properly.
Humor is finding the funny part of the events that happen without putting anyone down.
Also, don't take yourself too seriously. Give yourself, including your children, permission to laugh. Laughter is a great healer!
Without humor, life can be a terrible burden! Laughter is the best medicine!

WHEN YOU GIVE THESE GIFTS TO YOU CHILDREN, YOUR INNER CHILD INCLUDED, YOU OPEN THE DOOR TO A GREAT LIFE!

2. Sexual Relations

Sexual relations are the instinctual behavior of interacting sexually. This includes feeling or being attractive, how you dress and/or flirt, feeling fulfilled and/or achieving climax, to have intercourse and the capability to procreate --- being potent and fertile.

Procreation is part of the instinct. Courtship, preceded by

flirting, is a way to attract a mate with whom it may be possible to procreate. This is also the case with animals. Courtship is a way we ask for sexual relations.

Example: The peacock's courtship dance is to attract the female. Human dancing can be part of courtship, like the peacock.

When I was single I flirted a lot with different males. Now that I am married, I flirt amorously only with my husband. *Especially, if I want to have sex!*
Sex is the vehicle we use to procreate and establish total oneness with our mate, or simply satisfy our lover and ourselves.
The need to procreate is inside us at the instinct level. Probably the closest thing to immortality we can feel is through our children. We continue to exist by passing the genes, so in essence part of us continues to exist. The best example of this is the salmon that swims against the current to lay eggs. At the instinct level, she is willing to die to pass on her genes.

The Story of My Pregnancies

All my life I said I was not going to have children unless I had the right partner. My husband and I did not want to have children until we were financially ready.
At age 38, I got pregnant accidentally for the first time in my life, and my husband and I decided it must be God's will for us to have the baby. Unfortunately, I had a miscarriage and lost the child.

As a result of this pregnancy, and my connection with my instincts, I felt an urgency to have a child at age 39. I felt my biological clock was telling me time was running out. If I was going to have a child, it had to be now.

We discussed my need of having a child at this time, because we might not have the opportunity later. My husband agreed. I proceeded to try to get pregnant again.

I got pregnant one more time. One day, while walking my dog, I had another miscarriage. Then right after that, we tried once more, and I was three months pregnant when the doctor discovered the baby had no heart beat. I was sad to learn I needed a forced miscarriage.

After the third miscarriage, the doctor came to the conclusion that the problem was I was not creating enough female hormones to hold the baby. He also indicated what I needed to do was to get pregnant one more time and visit his office immediately thereafter for hormone shots to help the baby grow. By this time, I was not able to become pregnant. My age now was 42, so I decided to visit a fertility clinic.

While having a physical with the fertility doctor, he discovered a lump in my breast. The doctor said there was nothing he could do while the lump was there, and he referred me back to my primary physician. The breast lump now became a matter of life and death and thank God it was only Fibrocystic Breast Disease. With some research I discovered that Fibrocystic Breast Disease is very common with women going through menopause.

During this period, I asked God, "Why the lump in my breast?" The answer was very clear. The breast represented mothering, including nurturing. I was so obsessed with having a child that I developed a lump in the area that represents mothering. Also, I realized I needed to forgive myself for not having planned to be a mother sooner. With the combination of forgiving myself, listening to health and healing tapes, visualizing the lump gone, eating a proper diet, and taking vitamins, the lump disappeared.

I went back to the fertility doctor, only to discover my eggs were too weak and old, and the only way I could get pregnant was through an egg donor. The idea of an egg donor was not pleasant to me. Instinctively, I felt this was not right for me.

I questioned God again, "Why don't I want an egg donor?" I was directed to my instincts. I asked myself, "Why do I want to be a mother?" The answer was I wanted to procreate.

Procreation is God saying, "Make an extension of you, so that when you are gone, you continue to be here." I wanted a piece of me to continue to exist. That is the reason I rejected an egg donor. I understood to satisfy my maternal instinct, it did not matter if it was my egg or not. As soon as I realized this, my need to give birth to a child disappeared.

To satisfy the maternal instinct the Universe provides an abundance of opportunities. I can be maternal, loving, and nurturing with my husband, nieces, nephews, and pets. Another option could be adoption; after all, there are many children who need a loving home.

Flirting

What is it?

According to the dictionary, flirting is to act amorously without serious intentions.

Follow Your Instincts

Do you flirt?

Of course you do, but you might not be aware you are doing so. You flirt because it is part of your instinct. Intentional flirting, however, requires a degree of assertiveness, and its purpose is not necessarily concerned with the desire for a relationship. It could be to receive a pleasant acknowledgement from another party at a time that you may not be feeling so good about yourself. It could be as simple as a woman polishing her nails to advertise attractiveness. Also, a person dressing in a noticeably attractive manner is an automatic and subtle way of flirting.

Flirting is not necessarily romantic. Flirting could be an act of kindness. For instance, a woman might flirt with a very elderly gentleman to make him feel young.

Flirting is saying - I am here!

Dating

Dating can be a part of sexual expression. It is an exploration of compatibility.

Some of the games we play, as children are a preparation for adulthood. For example, the game hide and seek is a practice for future dating in adulthood. It seems it does not matter what part of the world the children are from, or what culture they belong to, this game can be found worldwide.

Have you ever seen adults play the game of saying no, when they are really interested in the other person? This is part of the hide-and-seek game you played as children. The reason the person says no is to become more important and interesting.

The more confident a woman is with herself, the more of an expert she is at the game of hide-and-seek. Some men will become experts at not giving up that easily.

Survival of the Fittest

Have you ever seen two males fighting for a female (or vice versa)?

From the instinct's point of view it is natural and okay! It is survival of the fittest.

Look at the deer, for example. When mating season arrives, males fight for the right to mate with the female. The female instinctively chooses the strongest male for security and to have the healthiest offspring. The reason is to have the stronger gene for the continuation of the species. This is called natural selection.

Women also choose men for security, comfort and procreation. In the middle ages the sword represented strength and security. Today's sword is money, which represents security. Women should not feel guilty about seeking a man who is financially secure. However, unfortunately many women over-emphasize this particular aspect. That should not be the primary factor for establishing a relationship.

Romantic perfectionism can affect your expectations. For men, it can create too much pressure to behave romantically. For women, it can stop them from choosing a particular male who could otherwise be a good mate.

Sexual behavior is determined by many factors such as, society, family, peer group pressure, and culture. Soap operas, TV shows, and other media have programmed us to think that without the proper goodies, such as expensive cars and fancy restaurants, we cannot successfully have a romantic relationship.

The truth is there is absolutely no criteria as powerful as that of presenting your true Self.

The prince on the white horse does not exist!

The Intellectual Connection of Sexuality

Man, with his intellect, has realized that anticipation (romance) lends as much excitement to sex as the actual act. Realizing that your brain is the most important sexual organ you have, communication between the two parties then becomes the primary tool in attaining an intimate satisfying sexual relationship.

Unfortunately, human behavior is not always what it should be, and in some instances there is a dark side to sexuality, and it appears in the form of sexual abuse.

What is Sexual Abuse?

Sexual abuse is any sexual experience an individual has that gets in the way of the development of healthy sexual responses or behavior. For some people, even one traumatic experience is enough to affect their sexuality and disconnect the person from their instincts. When there is sexual abuse as a child, the development of healthy sexual responses and behavior is affected. A nurturing and understanding partner can greatly assist in overcoming prior negative experiences.

Include in your sexual relationship communication, honesty, loyalty, trust, mutual respect, openness, laughter, and willingness to solve problems together.

Beliefs and Sexuality

One self-destructive belief is that you must take care of your partner's feelings, needs, and demands above yours. You may feel obligated to please your partner because of fear of rejection, if you do not meet his or her needs or demands.

If you have a headache, it is okay to say, "Not tonight dear, I have a headache!" But do not use it as an excuse. If you do not feel like it, it is okay to just say "no". *Sex should occur when both parties want it!*

One of the secrets to enjoy sex is to eliminate the pressure on both sides to perform!

Man, with his need to express masculinity, has been driven to aggressive behavior, separating himself from the caring and nurturing part of him (the female energy).

If you allow your feelings to get trapped, because of fear of non-performance or rejection, this will create an intimacy barrier.

In a sexual relationship, when a woman behaves assertively by taking the initiative of asking for what she wants, she is not only creating intimacy for herself, but also releasing her partner from the expected role of making the first move. Her acting assertively allows the couple to equally share in the expression of intimacy.

It is important to notice intimacy can occur without sex being present! The only way intimacy can occur is if you are open and honest with what you are feeling.

There is a difference between sex and lovemaking. Sex is sex. Lovemaking is the total physical, emotional and spiritual joining of two committed partners - total intimacy.

SUMMARY

Sex instinct, your sense of male and female, and everything involved with your sexual interaction, is composed of two parts: sexual identity and sexual relations.

1. Sexual Identity

Sexual identity is your sense of yourself as male or female, your sense of being maternal or paternal, feeling attractive or attracted, and feeling stimulating or stimulated.

Your sexual identity is your understanding that you have male and female hormones and for that reason, you have qualities of male as well as female within you. One becomes more dominant than the other, making you a male or a female.

2. Sexual relations

Sexual relations is the instinctual behavior of expressing and interacting sexually. This includes feeling

Sex Instinct – Sexual Identity and Sexual Relations

or being attractive, how you dress and/or flirt, feeling fulfilled and/or achieving climax, to have intercourse and the capability to procreate --- being potent and fertile.

Procreation is part of the instinct. Courtship, preceded by flirting, is a way to attract a mate, with whom it may be possible to procreate. This is also the case with animals. Courtship is a way we ask for sexual relations.

The sex instinct has to do with your sexual identity and your sexual relations. Being in touch with this instinct will result in a fulfilling sexual life.

Embrace your sexuality; it is God's gift to you!

Making love, and having sex is part of your instinct!
Enjoy!

We honor ourselves and our friends when we can tell them how we feel.

- Theodore Isaac Rubin

Chapter 5

BE ASSERTIVE AND FOLLOW YOUR INSTINCTS

What is Assertiveness?

Assertiveness is the ability to express yourself and your rights without violating the rights of others. It is done at the appropriate time in an honest, open, and direct way.

According to the dictionary, assertiveness is:

1. To state with assurance and confidence
2. To maintain or defend a position
3. To state as having existence
4. To postulate

Assertiveness reflects genuine concern for everybody's rights.

By learning to become assertive, you reduce the anxiety you may feel in dealing with others.

Research has demonstrated that developing the ability to stand up for yourself and doing things on your own initiative, can cut down your stress and increases your sense of worth. Consequently, you will improve your self-confidence and self-esteem.

Follow Your Instincts

What happens is that most of us have been trained to act either passively (be nice), or aggressively (get what you want), instead of being trained to be assertive.

Passive and aggressive behaviors fail to get you what you want. The objective of this chapter is to assist you in becoming more assertive.

Assertive behavior helps you build closer relationships because as a result of being assertive, you express your honest feelings and respect the rights of others.

When some of us were children we were trained not to be assertive when we tried to express our feelings, and we were told things like the following:

1. Do not talk to your father (mother) that way. You have to respect your parents. Never speak up to your parents.
2. Children are supposed to just listen, not speak.
3. I never want you to talk like that again.
4. Children have to be respectful to adults no matter what.
5. Never talk back to your superiors. (These superiors are what I call the "big people" in a child's life, like a parent, grandparent, school teacher, priest, rabbi, etc.)

No wonder some of us have difficulties becoming assertive!

The old style of teaching seems to have been one of the negative factors that hindered assertiveness. They usually rewarded the "well-behaved child". Quiet and well-behaved children did not speak up to adults.

Be Assertive and Follow Your Instincts

These messages told us we could not express our opinions and feelings, consequently, not allowing us to develop assertiveness skills.

Another message I heard while growing up was, "Turn the other cheek." What this phrase said to me was to not be assertive, but to be a doormat. Nonsense! If people are hurting you, it is your God-given right to become assertive and to set boundaries. When you allow yourself to be assertive, you will be of greater service to others as well as yourself.

There are certain patterns of thinking which make assertive behavior more difficult to achieve, such as:

1. The person we act assertive towards will not like us.
2. What will people think of me? They might even think I am crazy.
3. I might make a fool of myself.
4. I will fail to get what I want.
5. I might get fired.

All of these thinking patterns are fears of possible consequences. Your fears will hinder your ability to be assertive. I will discuss fears in Chapter 7.

Assertiveness helps you act in your own best interest at home, at work, and in any situation you might find yourself. It allows you to stand up for yourself without anxiety. It allows you to honestly express your feelings in a given situation. It allows you to exercise your personal rights without affecting the rights of others.

Every time you act in your own best interest, you are raising your self-worth and your self-esteem. Most importantly, you are taking care of your number one relationship, the relationship with yourself. You will also find it will greatly enhance your relationships with others

Use Assertiveness to Stand Up for Yourself

To stand up for yourself includes having the ability to say "no," setting limits or boundaries with someone, responding to criticism, expressing, defending or supporting an idea or opinion.

Standing up for yourself and being assertive includes:

1. Expressing your feelings openly and honestly without reservations.
2. Exercising your God-given right to expression.
3. Respecting others' opinions and feelings.

If you want your feelings and opinions to be recognized, you have to accept and acknowledge the other person's opinions and feelings.

Assertive behavior is a positive self-affirmation. It contributes both to your personal life's satisfaction and the quality of your relationships with others. Ultimately, behaving assertively improves your self-esteem.

YOU HAVE TO BECOME ASSERTIVE WHEN NECESSARY, IF YOU WANT TO HAVE GOOD SELF-ESTEEM.

Three Behavioral Characteristics - Passive, Aggressive and Assertive

There are three ways in which you can behave:

1. PASSIVE
2. AGGRESSIVE
3. ASSERTIVE

Let's look at these three behaviors.

Passive Behavior

When you act passively, you give up your right to be honest with your beliefs, thoughts, and feelings.

Do you go through life giving in to the wishes and desires of others?

You act passively because you want to please other people and avoid conflict. However, the price you pay is you can end up feeling anxious, helpless, ignored, hurt, manipulated, disappointed and resentful towards yourself and towards the person you are pleasing.

Sometimes you might complain of headaches, stomach disturbances, general fatigue, rashes, and even asthma. All of these symptoms may be related to a failure on your part to act assertively, because you chose to act in a passive manner. On the other hand, if you learn to behave assertively, you will not only avoid all of these symptoms, but you will also gain health, and you will build your confidence. You will feel more capable, but more

Follow Your Instincts

importantly, you will develop a belief system whereby you can express your feelings and opinions.

When you act passively, you end up doing what other people want you to do, regardless of how you feel. You allow others to walk all over you. Also, when you behave passively, you are likely to think of an appropriate response after the opportunity has passed. This behavior will lead you to feel incompetent, usually, saying to yourself, "I should have said _____."

WHEN YOU ACT IN A PASSIVE MANNER, YOU ARE SEEKING TO PLEASE AND BE LIKED; OR YOU ARE AVOIDING CONFRONTATION.

Aggressive Behavior

When you act aggressively, you are acknowledging your beliefs, thoughts, and feelings, but you do this in a dishonest way, which almost always steps on the personal space or rights of the other individual. This is usually not helpful, because it involves blaming and threatening or fighting, coming from a place of anger and frustration.

When you behave aggressively, you feel controlling and superior, followed by feelings of embarrassment, guilt, and loneliness.

When you behave aggressively not only do you leave a negative impression on the other person, but also you end up feeling sorry afterward.

WHEN YOU ACT AGGRESSIVELY YOU ARE SEEKING TO PROTECT YOURSELF AND WIN. AT THE SAME TIME, YOU WANT TO HUMILIATE,

Be Assertive and Follow Your Instincts

DOMINATE, OR FORCE OTHER PEOPLE TO LOSE. YOU MIGHT DO THIS CONSCIOUSLY OR SUBCONSCIOUSLY.

Assertive Behavior

When you act assertively, you are acknowledging your beliefs, thoughts, and feelings by standing up for your personal rights in a direct, honest and helpful way without violating the personal space and rights of others. You express your needs clearly and keep the lines of communication with others open.

Assertiveness means respecting yourself, acknowledging your beliefs, thoughts, feelings, needs, and rights. It also means respecting the beliefs, thoughts, feelings, needs, and rights of others.

The nature of assertiveness is such that you cannot be assertive at the expense of someone else!

When you act assertively, you feel better about yourself and as a result, you will increase your self-confidence and develop better self-esteem.

Being assertive does not guarantee winning, but it will guarantee that your self-esteem will improve, and you will have a good chance of getting better results without making others angry at you.

The most likely outcome, when you behave assertively, is that you will often get what you want without hurting others. You gain self-respect, and feel good about yourself. It becomes a win-win situation.

Assertive communication is direct, open, and honest.

One of the benefits you will obtain from being assertive is reduced stress.

THE OBJECTIVE WHEN YOU ACT ASSERTIVELY IS TO COMMUNICATE AND BE RESPECTED BY ACKNOWLEDGING AND EXPRESSING YOUR FEELINGS. YOU AVOID THE LONELINESS THAT CAN BE EXPERIENCED WHEN YOU ARE EITHER UNAWARE OR UNABLE TO EXPRESS YOUR FEELINGS.

How Others Feel When You Behave in a Passive, Aggressive, or Assertive Manner

When you act in a passive manner, people feel irritated, frustrated, and disgusted with you, and they lose respect for you because they feel they can step all over you. They end up pitying you, but most importantly, they end up manipulating and controlling you.

When you act in an aggressive manner, people feel hurt and angry. They become defensive and resentful. They distrust and/or fear you, and most of the time they will want revenge.

When you act in an assertive manner, people usually respect, trust, and value you. They know where you stand.

An example:

A dog is a great example of the use of assertiveness to protect his personal space. If a dog feels someone is coming to attack the pack, the first thing it will do is bark

Be Assertive and Follow Your Instincts

as a warning signal. He is saying, do not come any closer because I am prepared to protect my personal space.

I own a dog, and when I am in the car and a person is running nearby, he immediately begins to bark. Running in the wild represents danger. Therefore, when my dog sees someone running, he interprets it as danger.

Different Situations May Require Different Behavior

You may sometimes act passively, other times aggressively, and still other times assertively, and on each one of these occasions you might be acting in the correct manner, depending on the situation.

For example:

> 1. If a robber puts a gun to your head that may not be the right time to be assertive. It may be in your best interest to be passive.
>
> 2. If a policeman stops you to give you a traffic ticket, this is almost always the time to be humble and passive.
>
> 3. If a mugger attacks you, it might be prudent to be aggressive and overpower him if possible. In this case, aggressive behavior becomes an asset.

Choose your battles carefully, and weigh the cost against the benefits of being passive, aggressive, or assertive.

Follow Your Instincts

Your instincts will guide you as to what is the most appropriate behavior all time. In other words --- *follow your instincts.*

Five Ways to Become More Assertive

1. Plan your assertiveness.
2. Visualize yourself being more assertive.
3. Role play your assertiveness. Imitate someone you know who acts assertively.
4. Get some support, and ask someone, like a friend or a family member, to encourage and help you act in an assertive manner, most importantly, by praising you whenever you are assertive. This will help re-enforce your continued practice of this behavior.
5. Reward yourself when you succeed in being assertive. Do something nice for yourself.

Benefits of Being Assertive

Some areas that will be improved as a result of acting assertively are:

1. You will increase your self-esteem.
2. You will increase your connection with your intuition, experiencing better results from following its guidance.
3. You will express your opinions.
4. You will make requests.
5. You will think well of yourself.
6. You will respect yourself.
7. You will make decisions.

8. You will create limits to help you give to others.
9. You will be able to establish healthy boundaries.

The Art of Saying "NO" Clearly

In learning to be assertive, you have to learn to say, "no." For some of us, saying "no" can be very difficult, especially if we are people-pleasers.

When you say "no," try not to apologize because when you apologize, you weaken your position, and you make yourself open to being manipulated.

A tool I used was to practice saying "no" in front of a mirror. The next time you have to say "no," you might want to use this tool.

When you stand up for yourself, and say "no" when necessary, the result is improved self-esteem!

Another thing is that after you say "no," you might feel guilty. That is okay. The guilt will eventually disappear. The benefit is that you will feel good about yourself, and as a result you will increase your self-esteem.

Remember, nothing is written in stone. You have the right to change your mind and refuse a request you may have agreed to before.

If someone reacts to your assertiveness by being verbally abusive or aggressive, you can use the power of silence. *It takes two to tango!* If you do not argue back, the other person is powerless over you. This too is a form of assertiveness.

Follow Your Instincts

Silence is a very strong form of communication!

Achieve Success by Applying Assertiveness

When you apply assertiveness to *follow your instincts* you are automatically a success.

I remember one time I was at a business meeting and the subject of the meeting was lost because one particular person continually guided the meeting away from its initial purpose. By following my instincts and acting in an assertive manner, even though I was not the chairperson, I exercised my right to comment by firmly suggesting we get back on track and continue with the meeting's original purpose. Once again, assertiveness saved the day!

Assertiveness at the Gas Station

I remember another time, entering a gas station to fill up. I was cut-off by a lunch truck as I approached the pump. I turned around and went to an unoccupied pump and proceeded to the cashier to prepay. The same driver tried to get ahead of me in the line. Being assertive, I told him it was not nice to cut people off and that this was his second offence. He remained silent at the counter, but on the way to the pumps, he insulted me with improper, foul language. I chose to be passive to avoid a confrontation. He continued with his unpleasant behavior until I went to the other side of the car, retrieved my guard dog, and quietly returned to the task of filling up my tank. With my dog at my side, I assertively said to him, "If you do not stop, one command from me is all my dog needs." Needless to say, he immediately entered his vehicle and drove away. *Score one for assertiveness!*

As you can see, there are times when the use of passiveness and assertiveness has their appropriate place. If it became necessary, I could have also exhibited aggressiveness and commanded my dog to protect me.

The little victories in life count, not only the big successes. In this example, being assertive made me successful for that day.

SUMMARY

Assertiveness is the ability to express yourself and your rights without violating the rights of others. It is done at the appropriate time in an honest, open and direct way.

Assertiveness means respecting yourself, acknowledging your beliefs, thoughts, feelings, needs, and rights. It also means respecting the beliefs, thoughts, feelings, needs, and rights of others.

Every time you act assertively, you are raising your self-worth, self-confidence and your self-esteem. Most importantly, you are taking care of your number one relationship, the relationship with yourself. You will also find it will greatly enhance your relationships with others.

Success is how you feel inside.
Assertiveness will lead you to that feeling.

To err is human, to forgive divine.

- *Alexander Pope*

Chapter 6

LEARN ABOUT ANGER AND ELIMINATE RESENTMENTS

Anger – A Misunderstood Emotion

When we were children, we were trained that having or feeling anger was bad. We were told not to express our anger, and that we needed to be good at all costs.

Anger is a signal from the Universe that something is wrong. Anger might be a signal that we are being hurt, that our boundaries might be affected by someone else's behavior, that our needs and wants are not being met or paid attention to, or it might just be a big signal from the Universe (God) that something is wrong.

Anger is something you feel because the Universe built it inside you. For this reason, it deserves your full attention and respect. You have a right to your feelings, including anger.

According to the dictionary, anger is:

1. A feeling of displeasure resulting from injury, mistreatment, opposition, etc., and usually showing itself as a desire to attack back at the supposed cause

of the feeling.
2. Pain or trouble.

Anger was implanted at birth as a message that some corrective action is probably necessary. It is an aid to functioning in society. It is part of self-preservation and a protective mechanism against being hurt. Suppose someone attacks you physically, anger will help you fight back and defend yourself. This attack could also occur on an emotional and/or spiritual level.

Anger is the feeling we get when we believe someone has hurt us. It is an alarm that something might be wrong. It is the emotion that helps us defend ourselves when we feel attacked. Anger goes off inside us automatically without our permission. When someone invades our territory (physical, emotional, or spiritual), anger is the signal to do something about it.

Anger can help you protect yourself from a relationship where your beliefs, values, and desires are not being attended to. Your anger might be signaling that you are giving too much to a relationship and forgetting yourself.

Your anger can be your best friend, protecting you from the pain that others might cause you. Just like physical pain is a protective mechanism, (for example, if you put your hand on a hot stove, pain is going to make you remove your hand), anger is also a protective mechanism. It is important to not be ashamed of having this feeling.

ANGER IS NEITHER CORRECT NOR INCORRECT, ANGER IS SIMPLY A MECHANISM THAT INDICATES — **STOP** — SOMETHING IS WRONG. SEE WHAT IS WRONG AND CHANGE IT.

Questions that you might ask yourself to find out what wrong was done to you:

>What did they do to me?
>What did you do to me?
>What did my parents do to me?

Find out what is underneath anger.
>Is it hurt or pain? — Is it fear or self-doubt?

Face Your Anger

When facing anger, ask yourself the following questions:

1. What is my anger telling me?
2. What am I really angry about?
3. Is my anger legitimate?
4. Is this my problem or the other person's problem?
5. Is my anger telling me something needs to be changed?
6. Do I have to remove myself from a particular person or situation?

When you get angry, depending on circumstances, it may be best to wait for a cooling-off period. Then, analyze your position before you express how you feel. Here are some suggestions:

1. Analyze the situation.

2. Call a friend to help you find out what might really be troubling you about the situation.

3. Find out which instinct is being affected.
4. Write about the situation.
5. Meditate and ask God for the answer.

Talking to a friend can be a great way to become aware if you are feeling angry instead of hurt, or feeling sad instead of depressed. Once you connect with the true feeling, you can find a practical solution by asking yourself the following questions:

1. Are my needs or wants being affected, or perhaps is it that I think they will not be met?
2. Am I afraid of something?
3. How can I express my needs and wants without becoming defensive or offensive?
4. What boundaries, if any, are being violated? Do I have to set a boundary?
5. Am I trying to control someone or a situation?
6. More importantly, how can I express my anger in the best way possible for both parties involved.

You see, if your anger is telling you that you need to set a boundary, and you do not do it, what will occur is you will end up resenting yourself for not taking the proper action. Since resenting oneself is difficult, most likely what you will end up doing is resenting the other person. You transferred the pain to someone else, *so you think!* In reality what happens is you now have twice as much pain as before, the pain of resenting yourself, plus the pain of resenting the other person. The only thing is you are not aware of it.

Anger and Boundaries

Some people do not respect boundaries. This might require you becoming assertive with that person. For example: Let's say a co-worker sits at your desk and touches some of your personal papers without your permission, and you get angry.

Let's analyze this. What is your anger telling you?

Most likely your anger is telling you that you have to set a boundary and tell your co-worker not to sit at your desk and not to touch your personal papers.

If you do not set boundaries for fear that your co-worker will get upset with you, or that he or she might dislike and/or disapprove of you, you will be allowing him or her to continue with the same behavior. You will continue to get angry and eventually develop resentment toward that person. But let's be truthful, who are you really angry with? Most likely, you are angry at yourself for not setting the boundary with your co-worker.

From this example, we can conclude that anger is a healthy signal from the Universe telling us something is wrong. Go and fix it!

To connect with what I need to change, I use the serenity prayer, which is as follows:

> *God, grant me the serenity to accept the things*
> *I cannot change,*
> *The courage to change the things I can,*
> *and the wisdom to know the difference.*

I prefer to read the serenity prayer in reverse:

Follow Your Instincts

> *God, grant me the wisdom to see if there is something I need to change,*
> *If I have to change something, give me the courage to change it,*
> *and, if there is nothing that I need to change, then grant me the serenity to accept what I cannot change.*

The reason I say the serenity prayer backwards is that it helps me focus on what I need to change.

It might be difficult for some people to set boundaries for fear of rejection. However, once the fear is clearly understood, proper boundaries can be set. The next chapter will expand on fear of rejection, and how to handle it.

When you set proper boundaries, even at the risk of people not liking you, you are taking care of # 1 – YOU!

Anger and Relationships

Many of us have difficulty expressing anger for fear of hurting the other person and ultimately hurting the relationship. We might feel that expressing our anger might hurt the relationship, so we choose between having the relationship or having a Self. You cannot have a relationship, if you do not have your Self! The objective is to feel comfortable enough in your relationship to express your anger.

To achieve a healthy relationship, one has to be able to learn to express anger in a healthy manner. This might include instant notification of anger by your actions, followed by:

Learn About Anger and Eliminate Resentments

When you do _____, I feel angry because _____.

To achieve a long-term relationship you have to be honest about your feelings, and the other person has to be receptive of your feelings. Otherwise, it is a one-sided relationship and eventually it will not work.

A healthy relationship has three parts:

1. ME
2. YOU
3. US

If you are always angry in a relationship, it may require that you analyze which one of the three parts is affected. Is it me, is it you, or is it us? Have you ever started to express your anger only to get all confused about your feelings, and then began to apologize because you felt guilty.

The reason this occurred is because you did not pause to examine where your anger was coming from. It is best to know yourself and what you are feeling before you get into expressing anger. It is understood that sometimes anger is instant, and you do not always have the time to analyze it.

Anger is a tool for you to examine what needs to change in YOU. Anger is not for you to become an expert of the other person's behavior. Remember, the only person you can change is you and your attitudes.

Using anger effectively requires that you let go of the other person's behavior towards you and focus only on how that behavior is affecting you. It is important to stop blaming the other person. However, after having set the proper boundary, if that person continues with their behavior, the only solution may be to remove yourself from that person.

No one can make you angry without your permission. If you allow someone to get you angry, you have allowed that person to control you. The other person does not have the power to make you angry. Only you can make you angry. The anger is telling you to stop and analyze what it is you need to do. You are in control of your feelings.

Anger and Women

When you were a child, you were trained that feeling or expressing anger was bad, especially if you are a female. Girls were told they needed to be good at all costs.

If you are a female, to express anger is considered unladylike, unfeminine, and unattractive. I am here to tell you that anger is not bad; it is only a misunderstood emotion. How you express anger is what can be interpreted as good or bad.

If you are angry with someone for doing something to you, it does not give you the right to hurt him or her. However, it is healthy for you to express your anger as a form of communication, and it is your perfect right! This applies to all of us, male and female.

Suppressed Anger

Anger is a feeling, aggression is an expression of anger, and suppression is anger turned inward towards yourself. Some people are not able to feel anger as a result of having

Learn About Anger and Eliminate Resentments

suppressed their anger for a long time. Suppressed anger is the anger you feel, but do not express openly and directly.

A lot of us were trained that anger had to be suppressed at all costs. Therefore, we learned to block anger and turn it inward, experiencing feelings of depression, anxiety, lack of energy, guilt, and shame. I believe anger is a healthy emotion that should not be suppressed. We just have to find healthy ways to deal with anger.

The reason some of us have suppressed anger is because of fear of rejection or the consequences it might generate. For example: if you get angry with your boss, you might suppress your anger for fear of losing your job.

Another example is getting angry with your parents for something they did to you, but your belief system is such that you cannot feel anger towards them. To deal with your anger, you end up turning it inward.

Sometimes you do not allow yourself to get angry to avoid conflict. In turn, what you do is stay silent and turn the anger toward yourself, becoming self-critical and hurting yourself. Sometimes this anger directed inward will take you to drinking or overeating, or punishing yourself in another way. The result of not facing your anger will create pain and lower your self-esteem, because you are not acknowledging your feelings or yourself.

When you turn anger towards yourself because you want to be a "nice person," what you are really doing is putting the other person's feelings before yours. Does that make sense? Not to me. You have to learn to acknowledge your anger, learn to recognize it, and clarify with yourself where you stand with your feelings.

Transfer of Anger

Have you ever been upset with one person and taken it out on someone else?

A parent may transfer anger from a relationship to a child. For example, if the mother or father gets angry with the other partner, he or she may transfer that anger to the child by criticizing, verbally or physically abusing, or just simply neglecting or rejecting the child.

If you experienced this abuse as a child, it might be difficult for you to identify it because of your love for your parents. It is important for you to resolve these feelings from your past in order to become whole.

Anger as a Result of Our Expectations of Others

Sometimes we feel angry or attacked, when others do not satisfy our desires. The truth is that often we place high expectations on others. When we think another person does not perform to our expectations, we may become frustrated, disappointed, and angry.

Frustration and disappointment are emotions we feel when we do not get, or think we are not going to get what we want. Sometimes frustration is a signal that we need to change the way we pursue and formulate our expectations of others.

We are the result of our life's experience. We must realize all of us do not have the same life experiences, therefore, we cannot expect everyone to react to circumstances the same way we do. Be kind and understanding.

The Fear Behind the Anger

When people make you angry you may experience negative emotions such as hurt, frustration, or disappointment. However, what is really behind these feelings is some sort of fear. The next time you get angry, ask yourself, "What is the fear beneath my anger?"

One of the reasons you may not express your anger is that you may be afraid of the reactions of others. More importantly, you may be afraid of the fear itself.

Sometimes you know a loved one will not withdraw their love if you express your anger, but you are still afraid of expressing yourself. Try to identify the cause of your fear. Once you have accomplished this, you might want to start your conversations by expressing your fear followed by the discussion of your anger.

Expressing your fear before your anger may make you feel vulnerable. Do it anyway. Honesty will lead you to being humble, which in turn will make it easier to express your anger in a rational manner.

When you are able to identify and express your true feelings (fear or anger or a combination of both), you are being true to yourself and others. This behavior will build your self-confidence, self-esteem, and improve your relationships. You are then connected with and following your social instinct, which is the relationship with yourself and others.

When you know you are dishonest about not expressing your fear and/or anger, you will feel guilty. This information will become clearer to you in Chapter 8.

Follow Your Instincts

You can start a sentence to express your fear followed by your anger such as:

1. I am afraid to talk to you about my anger; however, I feel I have to be honest and open with you.

2. I am afraid that if I tell you what I am angry about, you will get upset with me and – fire me – reject me as your friend – stop loving me.

3. I have to tell you something that makes me angry, but I am afraid of your reaction. May I be honest with you without the fear that our relationship might be affected?

Then, express your anger without accusing the other person. Something like this:

When you do this _____, I feel angry because _____ affects my _____ (define which instinct is being affected).

Only talk about you, not the other person.

Use Anger Constructively

First, understand what your anger is trying to tell you, then, think and plan how you are going to express it constructively. However, there are times when there is nothing wrong with venting your anger as long as you are not abusive to the other person in doing so. As a matter of fact, there are circumstances in which expressing your anger is necessary.

When you tell someone you are angry, you are putting him or her on notice that you are prepared to defend your position.

Sometimes to avoid confrontation when someone has violated you, you tend to blow up at a different person, instead of the person you are angry with. This creates two situations. First, you do not have the right to take out your anger on someone who is not the cause of your anger, and second, you deprive yourself of the opportunity to set the proper boundary with the offender. Only direct the anger towards the person who offended you. In that way, you might be able to correct the situation or stop the abuse.

When expressing your anger it is important to try to do it from a calm position. Sometimes this will require creating some distance from the source of the anger.

When faced with anger in the course of a conversation, in order to create some distance, you can say, "What you just said is upsetting to me. I am not sure of the reasons why, so I need some time to calm down. I want to discuss this later when I am calm." Or, "I will get back to you later." Also, when you speak to the person later, it is best to say, "I *feel* hurt and angry," versus, "I *am* hurt and angry."

Anger Can Become the Energy to Make Change

Anger can be a great tool to assist you to become clear about your priorities. It will help you determine your needs, wants, and values.

When you get angry, it is usually a need or a want being affected, or that you think might be affected in the future. Ask yourself, "What are my needs and wants? Are they being affected by this situation, or is it my fear that they will be affected?" Once you have an answer to these questions, you can proceed properly.

To be able to use your anger correctly, the first thing you have to do is be very clear of where your anger is coming from. You must know yourself. You must define what you think, feel, and believe. By knowing yourself, and getting familiar with your instincts, you will be able to know the difference between your needs and wants. Your challenge is to fully understand your anger and use it to help you change yourself, and the situation you are involved in.

ANGER CAN BE A POWERFUL TOOL FOR PERSONAL GROWTH.

Become Assertive and Express Your Anger

Once you have expressed your anger, it is time to set the boundary of what you need or want. Tell the other person clearly what has to be different. The objective here is not to try to change the other person but to be very clear about what you need or want.

Prepare to be assertive in the following ways:

1. Acknowledge your anger. Pause, if necessary to understand why you are feeling angry before expressing it.

2. Identify the fear behind the anger.

Then, begin the assertiveness process:

Learn About Anger and Eliminate Resentments

1. Express your anger to the person who offended you and not anyone else.
2. If you are afraid to express your anger, start the conversation by saying you are afraid.
3. Set the proper boundary by telling the other person what you want from them. Use the "I feel" approach, instead of the "I am" approach, and do not accuse the other person.

You will be surprised at the results of taking these steps. More importantly, you will feel better about yourself, resulting in increased self-esteem.

Sometimes it does not matter how respectful your approach is when expressing your anger, because some people may still get upset with you. That is okay, remember, your responsibility is to take care of # 1 - YOU!

Now, Let's Talk About Resentments

Anger is a temporary emotion. When you hear yourself saying, "I am angry" over and over again, you have turned the anger into resentment.

There is a universal law that says two items cannot occupy the same space at the same time. Resentment is a negative energy that blocks you from creating success, wealth, and happiness. You must let it go. Negative energy (resentment) has to be replaced with positive energy (God).

According to the dictionary, resentment is:

A feeling of displeasure and indignation from a sense of being injured or offended.

Resentments can teach us that we sometimes hate and love the same person. The reason for this is we love the person, but hate something the person does. For example:

PERSON	CAUSE
My wife/husband	Does not listen to me
Parents	Are always trying to influence my thinking
My boss	Makes me stay late

When you are able to separate the person from their actions, it is easier to identify the resentment. You can focus on what they do and see what part you are playing. In the example of the boss making you stay late, if you are honest with yourself, it is probably your fault you stay late, because you are not setting the proper boundary.

Resentment as a Result of the Confusion Between Needs and Wants

My friend Elizabeth called me to express the pain she was feeling about her parents not helping her move. "I resent them," she said.

So, I asked her, "What do you *need* or *want* from them?"

"I need help moving," she answered.

I explained it was clear to me what she *needed* was help moving. However, she *wanted* the help to come from her parents.

What she *needed* was to recognize the difference between her *needs* and *wants*. If she opened herself up to having her *needs* met, the Universe would provide her with help in another form. I suggested she call a mutual friend and ask for help moving in order to get her need satisfied. The moment Elizabeth recognized and understood she could ask someone other than her parents for help, the pain and resentment disappeared.

Another friend called me because she was upset her friend Ana no longer wanted to be her friend. I asked her, "What is your *need*?"

She could not answer, so I replied, "Your need is to have friendship, and as soon as you open yourself up to allow the Universe to present another friend, you will realize that you did not really need Ana's friendship. It was your *want* not your *need* that you were upset about."

It is important to know the difference between your NEEDS and your WANTS!

Dogs Also Suffer From Resentments

My German Shepherd dog (Champ) developed very bad arthritis, so I decided to take him to a veterinarian who performs acupuncture (which is the insertion of needles into specific points on the body to cause a desired healing effect). The veterinarian, who was highly recommended by a friend of mine, suggested a procedure called Gold Bead Implants (where a dog gets gold beads permanently implanted into the arthritic area). I proceeded with his recommendation.

I have a metaphysical belief that arthritis is caused by holding long-term resentments. On one of my visits to the vet, I commented that a dog having arthritis proves arthritis is a disease and not caused by resentments. The vet immediately replied, "Dogs can also suffer from past deep emotional pains." He believes most arthritic dogs he treats have the disease due to resentments. Thank God that as humans, we can resolve our past painful experiences, eliminate resentments, and hopefully avoid diseases like arthritis.

Forgive to Eliminate Resentments

"Forgive those who trespass against us." -- Have you heard this before?

Forgiving those who offended you will lead to a happy, fulfilled life without resentments. But how can you accomplish this?

There are several methods that can be used to eliminate resentments:

1. Have a conversation (if appropriate) with the other person. If not, you can have an imaginary conversation by imagining they are in front of you, and you can say something like:
    I forgive you for _____.
    I've held resentment against you for _____, and I am forgiving you for that.
    I forgive you for how you treated me, and I ask for you to forgive me, if I offended you in anyway.

2. Write a letter to the person who offended you, but do not mail it. Write down what they did and how you felt. Then destroy it by burning or cutting it up. This technique

will help you put resentments in writing and eliminate negative feelings about the person you resent.

3. Pray to God for assistance in eliminating the resentment.

4. Meditate and visualize the other person getting everything they want, including similar good things you want for yourself. You can achieve this by visualizing the person you resent on a theater stage. Then, begin to send the person objects you think he or she would want, or send them what you want for yourself. For example, if you want a brand new car, you can visualize driving the car on the stage and turning the car keys over to that person. Begin to see how happy they are with your gift. Continue to give them presents until the feeling of resentment is gone.

5. Speak with a counselor or therapist. It does not matter what method you use; the objective is to eliminate the resentment. The main reason for eliminating resentments is they hurt us instead of the person we resent. It is easier to forgive others when we understand that sometimes we may have violated someone and needed forgiveness ourselves.

Forgiveness - The Path to Peace of Mind and Happiness

Your mind is like a projector to the world. When your mind is filled with anger and resentments that is what you will project, leaving no room for happiness and inner peace. You can choose to wake up in the morning and see a happy, friendly, and peaceful world. *Happiness and Inner*

Follow Your Instincts

Peace is an Inside Job! If your thoughts (cause) are of happiness and inner peace, then you will create that in your world (effect).

Becoming free from the pain of holding grudges and resentments is essential to achieving happiness. Remember, negative energy and positive energy cannot occupy the same space. Happiness and resentment cannot co-exist. Allow the negative energy of resentment to be replaced by forgiveness.

It is important to understand that forgiving is something you do in order for you to feel good about yourself. It has nothing to do with the other person. Forgiving someone is not looking for the other person's approval. Forgiving does not mean that we accept or tolerate what the other person did to us. Quite the contrary, in forgiving we are saying, "What you did to me hurt and you were wrong in doing it; however, I have resented you long enough, and it's time for me to heal myself, so I forgive you."

There are times you do not want to let go of the resentment or grudge. Facing the fact that you are resisting eliminating a resentment will help you let it go. You must be honest with yourself about the fact that you still want to hold on to the resentment or grudge, and that honesty might be the key that will open the door to let go of the resentment. *Honesty is the best policy!*

Other people do not have to change in order for us to have peace of mind. Forgiveness is one of the stepping-stones to that path. *Peace of mind is an inside job!*

The medicine for resentment and hatred is forgiveness. Forgiving will help you heal the pain, move on, reduce health risks, and enlighten your spirit. Forgiveness will **restore harmony with your family and relationships,** and

Learn About Anger and Eliminate Resentments

ultimately make you happy.

INNER PEACE AND HAPPINESS IS ACHIEVED AS WE FORGIVE OURSELVES AND OTHERS.

SUMMARY

Anger is a signal from God that something is wrong. Anger might be a signal you are being hurt. Your boundaries might be affected by someone else's behavior, or your needs and wants are not being met or paid attention to.

Anger is the emotion that helps you defend yourself when you feel attacked. Anger goes off inside you automatically without your permission. When someone invades your territory (physical, emotional, or spiritual), anger is the signal to do something about it.

If you are angry with someone for doing something to you, it does not give you the right to hurt him or her. However, it is healthy for you to express your anger as a form of communication, and it is your perfect right!

Anger is a tool for you to examine what needs to change in you. Anger is not for you to become an expert on the other person's behavior. Remember, the only person you can change is you.

Expressing your fear before your anger may make you feel vulnerable. Do it anyway. Honesty will lead you to

Follow Your Instincts

humbleness, which in turn will make it easier to express your anger in a rational manner to the other person.

Anger is a temporary emotion. When you hear yourself saying, "I am angry" over and over again, you have turned the anger into resentment.

There is a universal law that two items cannot occupy the same space at the same time. Resentment is a negative energy that blocks you from creating success, wealth and happiness. You must let it go. Negative energy (resentment) has to be replaced with positive energy (God).

Becoming free from the pain of holding grudges and resentments is essential to achieving happiness. Happiness and resentment cannot co-exist. Allow the negative energy of resentment to be replaced by forgiveness.

You can choose to wake up in the morning and see a happy, friendly, and peaceful world.

Happiness and Inner Peace is an Inside Job!

Learn About Anger and Eliminate Resentments

Here is a poem I have read and re-read over the years. I hope you find it as inspiring as I have.

People are sometimes unreasonable, illogical, and self-centered.
Love them anyway.
If you do good, people may accuse you of selfish motives.
Do good anyway.
If you are successful, you may win false friends and true enemies.
Succeed anyway.
The good you do today may be forgotten tomorrow.
Do good anyway.
Honesty and transparency make you vulnerable.
Be honest and transparent anyway.
What you spent years building may be destroyed overnight.
Build anyway.
People who really want help may attack you if you help them.
Help them anyway.
Give the world your best anyway.
The world is full of conflict.
Choose peace of mind anyway.

Anonymous

*You gain strength, courage and confidence by every experience in which you really stop to look fear in the face. You are able to say to yourself, "I lived through this horror. I can take the next thing that comes along."
….You must do the thing you think you cannot do.*

- Eleanor Roosevelt

Chapter 7

MANAGE YOUR FEARS AND ELIMINATE UNNECESSARY ONES

Fear is a state of mind.

If you want to be happy, successful, and financially secure, start by analyzing the fears that stand in your way.

A successful man is not one who does not feel fear, but one who is able to understand, manage, and overcome or eliminate his fear. The objective is not to fight the fear, or to hope the fear will simply go away, but to manage it.

According to the dictionary, fear is:

1. A feeling of anxiety and agitation caused by the presence or nearness of danger, evil, pain, etc.
2. A distressing emotion aroused by an impending pain, or danger, or by the illusion of such.
3. An alarm caused by a possible danger.
4. A painful emotional experience when a person is confronted by threatening danger.
5. Refers more to a condition or state than an event.
6. Often applied to an attitude toward something which, when expressed, will cause the sensation of

fright.

Fear is a God-given feeling to protect us from danger. It is present as a mechanism from the Universe to allow us to recognize in advance something might cause injury or death to us. It is a warning signal.

Fear could be an energy guiding you to action. Use this energy to empower you.

Fear is a feeling.   You feel hot.
                          You feel cold.
                          You feel hungry.
                          You feel angry.
                          You feel afraid.

Fear is a feeling, and it will not kill you!

In this book I only deal with normal fears not phobias. Phobias are obsessive or irrational anxieties.

What Are the Two Things You Need to Consider When Facing a Fear

1. Is the fear real?
2. Is the fear based on a need you think is not going to be satisfied?

First, make sure the fear is an indicator of a real or immediate danger. For example:

a. If you are trying to cross the street and a car is coming, you might feel fear. This is a real fear you must pay attention to. It is an indicator that if you cross the street, you might be hit or killed.

b. If a person is trying to rob you at gunpoint, you might feel fear. This is real fear. Your fear in this case is healthy. It is the way God communicates with you to help you survive.

Secondly, if you can clearly see that you are not in present danger, but you are feeling fear, then, it is a matter of recognizing a need or a want that may not be satisfied. *Real fear is a signal, warning you of imminent danger; the other feelings associated with fear are just thoughts, and can be changed.*

In the previous chapters we discussed instincts, and the difference between needs and wants. Being aware of the difference between your needs and wants becomes a tool to manage your fears.

Most of the time your fears are based on a need that you feel will not be satisfied at a future date. When you feel a fear ask yourself:

Which instinct do I think is not going to be satisfied?

Once you answer this question clearly, the fears will most likely subside.

Needs Versus Wants

One time a business of mine collapsed, and I was not able to meet my car payment obligation. The finance company called me almost every day threatening to repossess the car. Every time I received their phone call, I would get this knot in my stomach that would paralyze me. I used the need versus want approach, and I said to myself:

I NEED transportation — I WANT it to be this car.

The moment I realized my need was to have transportation to get around, I said to myself, "I could use my husband's vehicle (which was paid for). Moreover, if I needed some groceries (basic needs) I could go to the store on my bicycle." The moment I resolved the situation in my mind, I was in full control of my feelings and fears, and the phone calls ceased to make me afraid anymore. As a matter of fact, they ended up repossessing my car.

The two men, who came to repossess it, said to me, "You don't seem upset about the fact that you are losing your car."

"I am upset and sad that I am loosing my car," I replied, "but there is nothing I can do about this right now, and I am okay."

In order to understand which instincts are not going to be satisfied, you must become familiar with the three instincts previously described.

Another way to manage your fear is to ask yourself, "What is going to happen?"

Anxiety

Fears are usually in the immediate future. On the other hand, anxiety is a form of fear caused by not feeling capable of resolving now what is going to happen in the somewhat distant future. It occupies the block of time between now and the future!

Manage Your Fears and Eliminate Unnecessary Ones

When you are facing anxiety, you have to stop and ask yourself:

"What future event am I worrying about, and can I do something about it today?"

Anxiety is always related to a future event. When you find yourself anxious about something, see if there is something you can do now. If not, turn the problem or situation over to God.

What is the Difference Between Fear and Anxiety?

Fear is based on something that is happening now. For example: you see a snake in front of you. Anxiety is created by the thought of what might happen in the future, such as, thinking a snake will appear in front of you. Anxiety and fear produce the same physical reactions.

Most people suffer from spending too much time in the past or in the future, instead of being in the now. To be at peace with oneself, it is important to live continuously in the now. It is okay to plan for the future, but it is important to live in the present.

Anxiety is part of being human. As a matter of fact, a certain amount of anxiety is beneficial. Anxiety motivates people to figure out better ways of doing things.

Normal anxiety is positive. It is a mechanism from the Universe to warn you that perhaps there is something you should change or plan ahead to avoid future stress.

We worry as a mechanism to stop the things we are afraid of. For example, if the company you are working for happens to be going through a downsizing, you would be worried or afraid of losing your job. By worrying about it, you might find the energy necessary to go and look for another job, before you lose the one you currently have On the other hand, sometimes we worry over things that might never happen. When facing anxiety or worry, it is a good idea to look closely at the real reason for your concern. If you can do something about it, act on it. If not, change your thinking or replace worry with action.

Anxiety is worry - replace it with action. What can I do now to remedy that future situation?

Fear is an indicator that you should act with caution and do your best in any given situation. Fear is really preparation energy. It could help you get ready to excel, and do your best to learn all you need to know for a particular undertaking.

Fight or Flight Response.

When faced with a potential danger, humans as well as animals use the fight or flight response. This behavior is a response to fear. Our body automatically prepares to battle (fight) or to run away (flight). This is our built-in mechanism (adrenaline flow) to react to a perceived danger.

When an animal is threatened by the presence of a bigger animal, fear will cause the smaller animal to escape to avoid being eaten by the larger one. In this case, fear is a positive mechanism for the animal's survival.

Have you ever seen someone walk away from a discussion and even leave the room?

This person without knowing it, used the fight or flight response.

When the fight or flight response is triggered, the mind instantly analyzes all options and chooses the response.

Fear of Rejection

Fear of rejection creates worry. We worry about what is going to occur. This fear is based on wanting to feel safe. The world is a risky place, but we do not get ahead without taking risks. One of the reasons we are afraid to take risks is because we fear being rejected. Being rejected gives us a feeling the world is not safe, bad things can happen, or that we are going to look foolish.

If I have never been a waitress, do I have to get out of my comfort zone to be a waitress? The answer, of course, is yes. Imagine that you have never worked as a waitress, and you were just hired to be one. Your job is to serve customers including offering coffee and refilling it. Now, imagine that you go around the restaurant offering coffee to customers and people decline your coffee. After a while you would say, "I quit. I cannot take this job. No one wants coffee." If you do that, it is because you interpret the customers are rejecting you, instead of your coffee. If you, on the other hand, accept that part of being a waitress includes some customers declining coffee, then you will feel safe in offering coffee as part of your duties without taking it personally.

If we take this example into any other arena in life, we can conclude there will be rejection as part of whatever we might be trying to accomplish. To be successful, we must learn to embrace rejection instead of fearing it.

The more risks you take, the more you may be confronted with rejection. The more you face the possibility of rejection, the more you will be able to handle life on life's terms.

The reason behind fear of rejection is that you want to be accepted. Your self-image plays a big role in experiencing this fear. To avoid the pain of rejection, you will become a people-pleaser. The result will be a lower self-esteem and the loss of your self-identity in the process. This is a big price to pay!

The more you properly handle rejection, the better your self-esteem will be.

The best way to avoid the fear of rejection is through fear management. This requires a self-image that understands that not all people on earth will consider you and your talents to be the very finest. *If you are rejected, so what!* Don't let it stop you from taking risks and growing.

Fear of Failure

What will people think if we fail? The possible negative opinion of others is one of the biggest causes of this fear.

Failing does not make you a failure.

Failure is not the end of the world. We pick ourselves up, and learn from our mistakes. If at first you don't succeed, try and try again!

Sometimes we avoid failing by not placing ourselves in situations where we fear that might happen. If we are not willing to risk failure, we may never experience success.

Fear of failure is another reason why we do not take chances. *If you fail, so what!* If you do not take a chance, you do not have a chance! *Give yourself the opportunity to investigate life.*

My Personal Motivation Formula is:

NEED or WANT + FAITH = MOTIVATION

Faith is an unquestioning belief that does not require proof or evidence. Once you clearly identify your need or want, and mix in a healthy portion of faith, you will find yourself motivated. The Universe rewards action.

Make a list of all your successes, so the next time you have to take a risk and fear you may fail, you can look at your list and get some encouragement.

Success is a journey, not a destination!

One important thing to understand is that *failure is part of success, and it is an integral part of the learning process.* Failure is an aid to further progress.

Just go back in your mind to something you learned before. Did you fail a few times before you learned? A simple example is the first time you learned to ride a bicycle. Did you fall a few times before you finally learned to ride? Of course you did! We all did! So, why are we so afraid of failure? I believe it's because we fear what people are going to think about us.

Fear of failure produces a vicious cycle, which leads us to that which we fear, failure. To break this cycle you must make peace with failure by understanding failure is not your enemy; it is the stepping-stone that takes you to success. When you are trying something new, give yourself some room for failure and make those failures part of your success.

Success is going from failure to failure without losing enthusiasm!

Fear of Success

There are several reasons why people may think they fear success, but in reality they choose not to achieve success. In reality, there are three common reasons that cause the fear of success, and they are:

1. Not feeling worthy of success.
2. Fear of losing the success.
3. Fear of losing friends or loved ones, who may feel threatened by the success.

Fear of What People Might Think or Say

We live in society, and for that reason other people's opinions are part of our lives.

This fear has been very difficult for me to manage, as I'm sure it is for others. Although I understand it is important what other people think of me, I also understand this has to be taken in the right context. My actions cannot be controlled by what other people might think or say about me. How about you? In the final analysis, the only thing that really matters is what we think of ourselves.

Fear of the Future

This fear has a lot to do with not being in touch with your security instinct. You might worry about losing your health, your job or career, or not being able to meet your financial commitments. Once you can clearly identify the fear is based on thinking that the security instinct is not going to be satisfied, you can change your thinking and know it can be satisfied in the future.

Fear of Change

We all tend to resist change. However, one thing is for sure, the only thing constant is change.

Changing to a new pattern can be difficult! The experts tell us it takes 21 days to acquire a new habit. Therefore, you can say to yourself, "One day at a time, I can make it for a period of three to four weeks." Sooner than you think, a new habit is formed.

Fear of change many times can be attributed to feelings of not being in control.

Fear of Flying

It does not matter if you are a frequent flyer; most of us have experienced this fear to some degree. The reason is the terrible sense of vulnerability and not being in control. You feel helpless if anything were to go wrong with the plane. You have the power to change this thinking. Manage your fear by relaxing, and tell yourself positive affirmations. Trust the process.

Fear of the Unknown

The unknown can take us far from our comfortable present. Will we be able to cope? Only faith in ourselves will fortify us for the unknown challenges. The underlying fear is the possible removal from our comfort zone.

Fear of Loneliness

There is a difference between being alone and feeling lonely. Have you ever been in a room full of people and felt very lonely? Yet, you can be by yourself and not feel lonely!

You feel lonely when you feel apart from the world. When you have a sense of Self, you may experience being by yourself, but will not experience loneliness.

Some people have difficulty with this concept, especially if they have not developed a relationship with themselves. Some people feel they have to be with other people in order not to feel lonely. That is not true!

One of the best gifts you can give yourself is to become your own best friend. That way, you will always feel you have the best company anyone can have – YOU.

Fear of Losing Your Mate

When faced with jealousy, stop and analyze the three possibilities that might be driving you to this feeling. They are:

1. Low self-esteem
2. Possessiveness
3. An actual threat

Now, let's analyze an example of how each manifests itself.

Suppose you were just introduced to your mate's new secretary and you felt jealous. First, could it be low self-esteem telling you that you might be replaced? Second, could it be possessiveness, or the feeling you "own" your husband? Or finally, could it be an actual threat, and your instincts are giving you a signal to be aware?

To be able to discern the difference between these three examples, it is important for you to understand, connect with, and finally *follow your instincts*. If the message is from your instincts, then you must do something about it. Fear is a normal and protective reaction to an imagined or real threat.

Fear of Criticism

Some people do not take action toward their goals because of fear of negative messages they might receive. This fear can become a barrier to achieving success. For most of us, we are our own worst critic.

Fear of Poverty

If each thought has the power to translate into its physical equivalent, then, for example, fear of poverty, or thinking of being poor will lead you to poverty. This is true with the wealth mentality as well. Thinking wealthy will lead to wealth. Controlling your thought process about fear, will bring you to achieve great results.

Again, there is a universal law that states two items cannot occupy the same space at the same time. Thoughts are energy. The energy of your poverty thoughts cannot occupy the same space as your wealth thoughts. Decide which energy you are going to embrace. Fear of poverty can become the motivating force to make some people rich, if they channel this energy into a positive one.

Fear as a Result of Feeling Guilty

Sometimes guilt can be the cause of fear, if not a conscious level, perhaps at a subconscious level.

One Sunday, my husband was going to help his son change the kitchen cabinets, and I wanted to go on a boat ride with my dog Champ. I asked a girlfriend to accompany me because I was afraid to go alone. Saturday night I went to sleep afraid of what was going to occur the next day, for a reason I had not yet discovered. I even dreamed a shark was attacking my dog and me at the sand bar.

The next morning, I realized, I was facing two fears: One was the actual fear of driving the boat (since I had no experience), and the other was my fear of being attacked by a shark. In analyzing my fears, I recognized the fear of being attacked by a shark was the result of feeling guilty, because for the first time in ten years of marriage, I was going to go on a boat ride without my husband. As soon as I realized I was feeling more guilt than fear, the fear of being attacked by a shark disappeared and the fear of not being able to drive the boat became manageable. I took one step at a time and faced my real fear, that of not having enough experience to drive the boat comfortably.

Before arriving at the boat rental place, I asked God for help in facing my fear. When we arrived, they would not rent me the boat because I had no previous experience. At

Manage Your Fears and Eliminate Unnecessary Ones

that time I became disappointed, since my girlfriend and I had driven one and one half hours from Miami to the Florida Keys.

One more time I asked God what to do, and my eyes were directed towards an advertisement for small sand bar boat rentals. I asked the attendant if I needed experience to drive that particular boat, and he said no. I was very happy I was going to accomplish my goal.

My girlfriend and I rented the boat. I was still very afraid I might not be able to drive it in spite the fact the attendant said it was easy to learn. However, I faced my fear, started to drive the boat to the sand bar, and my confidence began to build. By the time we returned the boat, I was an expert. I felt great about managing my fear and *following my instincts*.

Fear of Loss

This is a very subtle fear that sometimes is difficult to recognize. When I was nine years old, we were going to leave Cuba on a freedom boat to escape the communist dictatorship. Not being allowed to take any of our possessions, my family gave all our belongings to friends and family, especially our clothing. Unfortunately, the boat never arrived. I suggested we ask for everything back, but my family said that once you give something to someone, you do not ask for it back. I remember saying to them that this was an unusual situation and that this rule should not apply. However, my family still would not ask for anything back. To my surprise, no one offered to return anything, which I thought was wrong. Unfortunately, we had to wait another four years before we were able to come to the

United States, making it a difficult period, since we did not have enough clothing.

The way fear of loss manifests itself in my present day life is that in order to be comfortable about my possessions, I try to take reasonable measures to prevent their loss by having most of them paid off. If by chance I were to lose something of value to me, then I understand that there must be a lesson to learn from the Universe.

Wanting Solitude but Fearing Loss

Sometimes letting go of a relationship can stir up fear of loss, as we are afraid of later regretting the decision.

My friend Christina was separating from her husband, but because of financial circumstances, they decided to stay in the same house for a period of time while each one prepared for the actual separation.

One day they went to a church gathering, and her husband began to flirt with another lady. She called me very upset because she could not understand her feelings. I asked her, "Do you really want to divorce your husband?"

"Yes," she answered.

I suggested she was experiencing fear of loss - fear that what she was letting go of still had a certain value to her, and later she might feel sorry for her decision. I suggested she needed to re-evaluate her decision. My friend realized that she had to take a chance and move on with life, and was finally able to let go.

Fear of Losing Your Job (Job Security)

This is the most popular fear. The best way to combat this fear is to increase your area of expertise, and become more competent. The more talent and knowledge you possess, the higher the demand will be for your services, and the more valuable you will become as an employee.

This fear is based in the security instinct. It is putting self-preservation in jeopardy that creates this fear. We all need food, clothing, and shelter to feel safe. The possibility of not having these items is what causes this fear.

Part of the security instinct is having talent, information, and opportunity. When these items are threatened, it can also be the cause of the fear.

Because the instincts are interconnected, and you cannot separate one from the other, this explains why one feels bad when losing, or has the possibility of losing, a job. If you feel bad about losing your job, you will feel bad about the relationship with yourself. In this case, if you feel bad about having lost your position, your social instinct will also be affected.

To take this explanation one step further, let's analyze how the sex instinct is affected in the case of losing a job. As an example: if you are a married man with a family and you lose your job, you may feel you are not a good provider, even though the circumstances may have been beyond your control.

The possibility of losing a job really affects all of your instincts: social, security and sex. *No wonder it is one of our biggest fears!*

Fear of Re-living the Past

We sometimes believe if something negative happened to us in the past, it will happen again in the future. This thinking process keeps us trapped in the past. Consequently, creating that which we fear.

Remember, thoughts are things. If you are thinking about something that occurred in the past, you will create it in the future. This fear can change and control your present behavior. To stop this vicious cycle of re-living your fears, every time you see yourself thinking about something that happened in the past and are afraid it will happen in the future, change your thinking. If you do not resolve the feelings from events of your past, then most likely the past will become your future. Stay constantly in the present, that way you are not in the past negative experience or in the fearful future.

Fear of Being at Home Alone

I have a friend who lives in a gated community and in addition has a sophisticated alarm system. Her husband needed to travel, and she was terrified to be home alone. She tried to control her fear to no avail. I suggested she get a guard dog, which she did, and her fear seemed to be less for a period of time.

On another occasion, her husband decided to go hunting, and she had to face her ugly fear one more time. Intellectually, she understood it did not make sense to have this fear since now she had triple protection: the gated community, the alarm, and the dog.

She prayed every night and asked God why she had this fear. Where did it come from, and how could she eliminate it? She finally arrived at the painful answer.

As a child her father had sexually assaulted her. However, she did not make the connection between this event and her present fear until now. Years before, in therapy, she dealt with the abuse, but never connected it with her fear.

Her father never actually raped her. The sexual abuse occurred by her father making sexual remarks towards her, and saying things like, "Look at your breasts, how big they are getting. Look at your butt. Now, you are looking like a woman." These two comments made her feel ashamed of her body, her femininity, and her sexuality.

She would be taking a shower and her father would walk into the bathroom. She remembers the fear she had being naked and feeling powerless. She told him not to come into the bathroom when she was there. He told her there was only one bathroom in the house, and he would use it whenever he pleased. Also, he would walk around the house in his underwear with his fly open. She was afraid of being in the house alone with him, fearing he would rape her at any time. This started when she was about eleven and lasted for a period of about seven years.

When she was able to connect her fear of being raped by her own father with the fear that someone would come into her home and actually rape her, she realized her fear was actually from the past. It was this awareness that freed her from the fear.

Some people, especially women, fear being alone because of the messages they have received from the adults in their lives, or simply from the news media reporting on break-ins, rapes and other violent acts. The way to deal with this fear is to first take all of the necessary precautions to protect oneself. Then, if the fear persists, use the power of affirmation to change your thinking, and ultimately ask your understanding of God for help. In the process, you may discover another underlying reason for your fear that you may not be aware of, like in the case of my friend.

Manage Your Fear via the Thinking, Feeling, and Action Process

Remember, fears are emotions that are a state of mind, which means you have the power to manage what you think. In turn, you can manage your fear.

When faced with a fear, go back to the thinking, feeling, and action process. You must change the thought that created the feeling of fear. If not, your fear will lead you to an action resulting in that which you fear. You have the power to control your thinking.

Peace of Mind as Your Primary Goal

Make peace of mind your most important goal each and every day. Your awareness of the present moment and your involvement in it will automatically put aside worries of the past and the future.

How many times did you worry about something you thought might occur in the future? Let the future be the future!

You can let go of fear and obtain peace of mind when you stop bringing forward the past and projecting it into the future. Live in the now!

Peace of mind is achieved by embracing positive thoughts and staying in the present moment.

Steps You Can Take to Manage or Eliminate Your Fears

1. Dedicate time to work on you. Self-knowledge combined with the use of your instincts will lead

you to a life free from fear. But as you know, this will not happen automatically - you must dedicate the necessary time!
2. Share your fears with another person. Sometimes you do not feel like expressing your fears because you do not want to make yourself vulnerable. Do it anyway!
3. Write about your fear to find the cause of it or at least to help reduce it.
4. Replace worry with action.
5. Let the future be the future. Half of what you worry about never occurs.
6. When facing a fear ask yourself:
    a. What could happen?
    b. Which of the three instincts do I think will not be satisfied in the future?
    Once you have an answer to these questions, you will be able to eliminate or manage your fear through understanding.
7. Ultimately ask God to help you eliminate or manage your fear by showing you where the fear is coming from.

SUMMARY

Fear is a state of mind.

Fear is a God-given feeling to protect us from danger. It is present as a mechanism from the Universe to allow us to recognize in advance something that might cause injury or death to us. It is a warning signal.

Fear could be an energy guiding you to action. Use this energy to empower yourself.

If you want to be happy, successful, and financially secure, start by analyzing the fears that stand in your way.

A successful person is not one who does not feel fear, but one who is able to understand, manage, and overcome or eliminate his/her fear. The objective is not to fight the fear or to hope the fear will simply go away, but to manage it.

Overcoming your fears will give you a new freedom and peace. Your entire outlook on life will change.

This is happiness!

Chapter 8

FREE YOURSELF FROM GUILT -- KNOW WHEN GUILT IS BEING USED TO MANIPULATE YOU

Guilt is the result of having a belief of how you should be, and your behavior not matching that belief. To free yourself from guilt, you either change your beliefs (thinking) or change your actions (behavior).

Guilt can become the energy for making personal change.

According to the dictionary, guilt is:

1. A painful feeling of self-reproach resulting from a belief that one has done something wrong or immoral.
2. The state of having done something wrong or committed an offense, legal or ethical.

Guilt is an emotion. Remember, emotions are feelings in motion. What this means is you must go back and ask yourself, "What was I doing that did not align itself with my belief system?"

Guilt is a signal that you may have violated your standards or the standards of someone else. Any time you violate your belief system or the standards you have set for yourself, you are likely to feel guilty. In either case, an amend changes the guilt feeling.

Sometimes we arrive at the conclusion that the standards we have set for ourselves are no longer worth keeping. In that case, it is easy to let go of the guilt. On the other hand, if we have decided to maintain our standards, then guilt is a signal that we have to change.

Have you ever spoken your mind and then felt guilty afterwards?

We usually want to be liked or accepted. If we did not really harm anyone, then the reason we feel guilty is our need for approval. This is important to know, especially if we are trying to be assertive.

What is the Difference Between Guilt and Shame?

Guilt is the painful feeling resulting from having a belief of how you should be and your behavior not matching that belief.

Shame is a painful feeling of having lost the respect of others because of your improper behavior. You believe that you are inadequate and/or somehow defective.

Although guilt and shame are both painful feelings, they differ in several ways. Guilt can be either diminished or eliminated by reparation or making amends. It has the possibility of being repaired. Shame, on the other hand, makes you feel you cannot ever reclaim respect no matter what you do because it implies there is something wrong with you or your family.

Know What Your Values Are

Every time you do something that conflict with your values or core beliefs, you will most likely feel guilty, thereby lowering your self-esteem.

Example ---- Your belief --- being faithful (value)
Your action --- being unfaithful
Your result --- feeling guilty

To achieve peace, you have to either change your actions or change your beliefs.

Some people would rather be confused about their values than decide what their values are, because while they are confused about their values, they do not have to take action.

Confusion is a great way to avoid responsibility.

Manipulation Through Guilt

What is manipulation?

According to the dictionary, manipulation is:

Manage or control by shrewd use of influence, often in an unfair or fraudulent way.

The manipulator is trying to control the outcome. When someone manipulates you, they are violating your personal space. This explains why you feel bad or angry when you feel manipulated.

Two phrases you are most likely to say to yourself that can indicate you have been or are being manipulated:

1. I should have ----
2. I shouldn't have ----

Some tools used by the manipulator:

1. Degrading you. For example, making you feel bad by using statements like:
    a. You are silly
    b. You are crazy
    c. You are stupid
    d. You are incompetent, etc.

By degrading you, the manipulator makes you feel inadequate, resulting in your doing what they want.

2. Playing upon your weaknesses. For example, if others know you have a fear of financial insecurity, they might strongly hint that unless you act in the manner they suggest, great harm and financial insecurity will be the result.

3. Playing on your need for attention, the manipulator will pick up on this need and give you the attention you desire. Then, he will control you with it. You will tend to do things for this person for fear he will remove that attention.

Connecting with your instincts will make you aware of your weaknesses. Listen to the messages you are receiving

Free Yourself from Guilt – Know When Guilt is Being Used to Manipulate you.

and the true intent behind them, and be sure the manipulator is not using your weaknesses against you.

The main objective of the manipulator is to control you.

The manipulator will identify a weakness in you; show you how he/she is going to help you with it, then control you with it.

I remember when I first started in real estate sales. I wanted to work in the commercial department selling shopping centers, apartment buildings, and other commercial properties. The company's owner manipulated me to work on other projects with the promise that he would give me commercial work in the future. The reason I agreed to do the work was because he said, "If you work on this project, the next commercial work is yours." I went on working from one project to the next never getting what I was promised. He manipulated me, or I allowed him to manipulate me, with the "carrot" that I was going to get the commercial work.

When you become aware, the manipulator is powerless!

Say "No" Without Guilt

Many times you allow the manipulator to control you because of your inability to say "no."

Have you ever found yourself saying "yes" to a situation you wanted to say "no" to?

The reason you say "yes" is to not feel guilty.

After you have said "yes," you might feel it is too late to back down from that position. You would feel guilty if you let the manipulator down.

When you say "yes" but really want to say "no", you feel guilty because you are not following your true instinctive feelings. Furthermore, you are not respecting yourself. Self-respect gives you the power to make your own choices. Other people should not decide for you. You decide for yourself.

What I have learned to do in situations where I am not sure if I should say "yes" or "no," is to say, "Let me think about it, and I will let you know." That way I do not commit myself. This allows me time to consider my decision and prevent the manipulator from winning.

Right now say "no" to yourself as if you were answering the manipulator. Now, don't you feel great and also guilt free?

Manipulation Via the Nice Person

Did you ever, on occasion, feel strange when someone was being too nice?

Probably at an instinctual level you knew the person was trying to manipulate you via the "nice person."

Guilt Cost George his Jaguar to the "Nice Girl"!

George met Nancy right after she arrived in his hometown. She was the epitome of the sweet little innocent young girl from somewhere in the mid-west. She became very active in his small close group, and attended all the

Free Yourself from Guilt – Know When Guilt is Being Used to Manipulate you.

local social functions, where it was frequently commented how nice Nancy was!

When I met Nancy, my instincts told me "beware" not to trust this person. So, I never got close to her. As time went by, I observed Nancy's manipulative ways with my friend George.

George is an easy-going successful gentleman, but not connected with his instincts, and therefore somewhat overly trusting of a pretty face. It was not too long before Nancy moved in with him into his oceanfront condominium, enjoying all the benefits his success could offer, while making him feel as though he had won a wonderful prize.

Nancy manipulated George, making him feel guilty that he had so much and she had so little. As time progressed, she began to be more demanding and George was reluctant to comply. Nancy then, in their close group, spread the word that George was being quite cruel to her, and asked her to leave his apartment.

The pressure George felt from his friends, being told he was a bad guy, and being asked how could he throw her out in the street, finally made my friend leave his own condominium.

The explanation for George's behavior is that it was easier for him to leave his domain, instead of dealing with his perceived guilt. In addition, he wanted to continue to have his friends' approval.

The final outcome of this situation was that George in exchange for the return of his home, and to prove that he was a good guy, gave Nancy his paid-for brand new Jaguar. What a price to pay! Sweet little Nancy did the same thing to another man just a few years later.

When we are not willing to analyze our feelings and eliminate unnecessary guilt, we can end up in situations like my friend George.

"Nice Girl" Almost Takes Gloria's Job...

My friend is a very successful art designer, and she needed an assistant. She hired Ana, who seemed to be a very nice girl at first. Gloria spent time training Ana and teaching her the things that were necessary to be her assistant.

Gloria works directly under the supervision of her boss, who is the owner of the business. Ana's job was to assist Gloria with the art design work, but unfortunately, her desk was outside of Gloria's office, together with the rest of the office personnel.

Ana saw an opportunity to perhaps get Gloria's job and began to manipulate everyone in the office via the 'nice girl act," bringing candy and pastries for everyone in the office. She began to organize happy hours with the rest of the office and not include Gloria. One time, she organized a dinner party with the entire office staff and did not tell Gloria until four days prior to the event. Gloria had to decline the invitation and was not able to attend the dinner. She had a prior commitment that, by the way, Ana knew about.

When Gloria spoke with me about this situation, I suggested that she had to let Ana go, otherwise Ana was going to continue to manipulate via the 'nice girl act'" and create more problems. I suggested that what Ana was trying to do was to first be this nice person, and then persuade everyone to be on her side. My friend was not able to fire

Free Yourself from Guilt – Know When Guilt is Being Used to Manipulate you.

Ana because she felt guilty. Ana was manipulating my girlfriend through guilt.

As time went on, Ana began to ignore Gloria. Even worse, Ana began to make Gloria look like a bad person in front of the rest of the office for telling Ana to do the work she was hired to do. Again, when my friend called me to let me know what was going on, I asked, "Who is the boss in this situation? Is she your assistant? Then, she needs to do whatever you tell her to do. I think it is time for Ana to go before she makes more trouble for you." Again, Gloria felt guilty about letting Ana go. I said, "I believe you are going to pay a very big price for not letting her go. In my life, there is no room for not being loyal. The first thing I demand from an employee is loyalty."

I went on to explain to my friend that Ana had no right to make her feel uncomfortable in front of her co-workers. Furthermore, if she did not become assertive and fire Ana, her job might be in jeopardy. Indeed, my friend learned a big lesson! Ana almost cost her, her job! Ana continued to manipulate to the point that Gloria began to have difficulties explaining to her boss why Ana was not doing her job. Gloria and her employer had never had any problems communicating for seven years prior. The entire atmosphere in the office was one of tension.

Finally, my friend, faced with the possibility of losing her job, became prepared to quit. She asserted herself and said to her boss, "It is either Ana or me. I cannot work with her." Her boss realized Gloria was ready to leave, and made the decision to let Ana go, after which the entire office returned to a peaceful atmosphere.

My friend learned several lessons. She learned that she needed to be assertive and do whatever the situation requires at the right time. If not, things might get worse. She also learned to be very careful with the "nice person act." Most importantly, she learned it doesn't matter if she feels guilty towards the other person; she must take care of number # 1 (herself) first.

BE CAREFUL YOU ARE NOT BEING MANIPULATED VIA THE NICE PERSON ACT.

Breaking Away From Parents Through The Release of Guilt

My friend Betty, who had always lived with her parents, allowed them to control her life. At age 34, after almost dying from coronary heart disease, high blood pressure, circulatory problems, diabetes, and a 100-pound weight gain, the doctors told her that if she did not make some changes in her life, she was going to die.

One day after coming back from the doctors, my friend suffered an identity crisis and began a soul-searching process. She discovered she felt like an extension of her mother. She had no clue where her mother ended and where she began. This realization made my friend want to become her own person and independent from her mother.

It took my friend four years in therapy and an understanding of her instincts before she was finally able to build enough courage to let her parents know she was moving out. Her mother did not accept the news very well and began to manipulate her into not moving by saying things like:

Free Yourself from Guilt – Know When Guilt is Being Used to Manipulate you.

- What would you do without me?

- You do not know how to raise a family.

- I cook and clean for you and your children will suffer without me being there.

- I save you money by sewing for you and your children.

- If you did not have me, your children would have to go to a day care center.

Betty's mother was manipulating her by making her feel guilty by saying, "How can you leave me when I do so much for you?" In addition, she was manipulating her by making her feel incompetent as a mother.

By the time Betty moved out of her parents' home, her children were already teenagers and she came to the sad realization that her mother had raised her children. She wanted to become her children's mother. By this time, Betty was in touch with her maternal instinct (sex), and when she spoke with me about her decision, I said, "Do not worry, your instincts will lead you to where you need to go with your children - just *follow your instincts*."

After my friend moved out of her parents' house, her mother began to give her guilt trips by saying things like:

- Now that I am old and I have raised your children, you do not need me anymore.
- You are now throwing me out like a dirty dishrag.

- I sacrificed so much for you and your children.
- You are most ungrateful.

These statements made my friend feel very guilty to the point of almost wanting to move back with her mother, so as not to deal with the guilt.

When someone else makes us feel guilty, even when we clearly know that we have not harmed them, and logically understand we are not the guilty party, we must feel the guilt and move on, like in the case of my friend Betty.

Call Your Mother — or Don't Call Your Mother

My friend Elizabeth called me very upset and crying one day because she was feeling guilty about having spent some years without speaking to her mother. I asked why she had decided not to speak with her mother. She explained that her mother would not respect her for who she was and every time they would speak, her mother would try to control her.

When unable to gain control, her mother would switch to making her feel guilty. Elizabeth explained that her mother always placed her male companions ahead of her. Some of these males even abused her, and her mother afforded no protection. Elizabeth said she needed her own space to heal and get strong before she could set the proper boundaries with her mother. She could not allow any of her mother's boyfriends to hurt her anymore.

I said, "If this was your decision, there is nothing wrong in not speaking with her for some time. The reason you were feeling guilty was because your belief system did not match your action. Everyone believes that daughters should honor their mothers!"

To achieve serenity and not feel guilty, Elizabeth had to change her action or change her belief. I said to my friend, "If you feel that you are a good daughter, even though you are not speaking with your mother, you have to either change your thinking (and believe it is okay to not speak to your mother), or change your action and call her"

Guilt Free Vacations

Did you ever go on a vacation and feel guilty you were having too much fun and your family was not with you? I did!

I used to get sick every time I took a vacation, until one day my husband said to me, "Have you noticed every time we go on a vacation you get sick?" This was very difficult for me to hear; however, I had to stop and analyze what he was telling me.

I discovered, that when I was a child, I was programmed with the idea that vacations were a total family affair, and we all went together. Because of my childhood programming, later on as an adult I felt that if I went on a vacation, I needed to take my whole family with me to be a good daughter, a good sister, etc.

The way I dealt with the guilt for not taking them along was getting sick. Of course, I did this at a subconscious level.

When I became aware of this thinking pattern, thanks to the help of my husband, I was able to change it and enjoy my vacations with my husband in absolute health and with no guilt.

I began to program myself with the following affirmation:

1. I deserve vacations in absolute health.
2. I am worthy of the best vacations.

Feeling Guilty About Not Feeling Guilty

I remember one day my mother called to inform me of the death of a family member. My mother wanted me to call the family and offer my condolences.

"I am sorry to hear this person died, but this news does not affect me, and I do not feel I have to call anyone," I said. I had made the decision that I did not want to be close to that person.

"How can you be like that? You do not have any feelings towards the fact that this person died?" she replied.

"I have feelings. I'm sorry she died," I answered.

As soon as I hung up the phone *I felt guilty for not feeling guilty* that this person died. I was also feeling terrible that I could be so cruel. This incident occurred during a period of time when I was dying of anorexia. I was feeling so guilty that I decided to set up an appointment with my therapist.

I explained to my therapist I was feeling bad for not having feelings about the person that died. My therapist explained it was okay for me to feel that way, and in no way did this mean I was a bad person, nor that I needed to feel guilty or feel bad. Furthermore, if I did not want to make that telephone call, that was also okay. What a relief!

Again, this is another example of how sometimes family members can try to manipulate us with guilt. My mother wanted me to call our family. She tried to make me do so through guilt. Of course, I do not think my mother did this to hurt me or anyone else. All she wanted was for her little girl to be good. On the other hand, at that time in my life, just dealing with my anorexia was a handful. Since at this time, I was not connected with my instincts, it was a miracle I had the intuition to *follow my instincts* and take care of # 1, ME. I did not feel like calling and I did not have to. If I had called to please my mother to avoid feeling guilty myself, I would have gone against my own feelings, resulting in lowering my self-esteem.

Don't Let Guilt Cause You to Continue in a Bad Relationship

Some people stay in a relationship because they feel guilty about leaving. Another reason is perhaps anticipating guilt because the family may not approve of ending the marriage. Perhaps, the guilt is deriving from concern about separating the children from the other parent. Whichever the case may be, guilt should not be the reason for staying in a relationship.

Guilt Through Dishonesty

Suppose you were thinking of getting divorced from your spouse, but you kept this information to yourself, fearing that if you were honest with him/her about your feelings, they would leave immediately under unpleasant circumstances. The guilt may surface in two ways: First, there is the guilt of acting in a manner wherein you are not being true to your belief system, such as concealing important information from your spouse. Secondly, there is the guilt of causing possible emotional pain to the partner.

In this situation, when you do not follow your true feelings and do not act in an honest way, you might develop self-anger. This can lead you to depression. On the other hand, when you honor your beliefs, even though you might risk upsetting your spouse or risk them leaving immediately, you will feel full of energy, and you will not damage your self-esteem.

No Regrets – No Guilt

The best way to keep yourself free of guilt is to not do those things that will cause you to feel it.

I firmly believe, having spoken with a number of people who have had near-death experiences, that when you face imminent death, it is not some of the things you have done that you regret, but rather those things you have not done. Would it not be wiser to do things such as being kind and loving to those around us while they are here with us on earth, rather than experience the guilt of not having allowed them the time, love, and attention while they were alive?

Feeling Guilty About Spending on Yourself

The reason you might feel guilty is that your belief is you do not deserve good things. This belief comes from a low self-esteem.

To improve, you can start by purchasing nice things for yourself and know that you deserve them. This behavior will increase your self-esteem and improve the relationship with yourself as well.

Free Yourself from Guilt – Know When Guilt is Being Used to Manipulate you.

Free Yourself from Guilt Through Forgiveness

Sometimes it is easier to forgive others before we can forgive ourselves. When we realize we too make mistakes and need forgiveness, it becomes easier to forgive ourselves and others.

Free Yourself from Guilt By Making Amends

When facing guilt, ask yourself, "Who did I harm?" If you did not harm anyone, then you have to let go of the guilt.

To eliminate guilt when you have harmed someone, your best course of action is to make amends. The amends list should include your own name.

You make amends to yourself living in accordance to the rules of the Universe. The spiritual life is not a theory. *We have to live it!*

SUMMARY

Guilt is the result of having a belief in how you should be, and having your behavior not matching that belief. To free yourself from guilt, you either change your beliefs (thinking) or change your actions (behavior).

Guilt is a painful feeling of self-reproach, resulting from a belief that one has done something wrong or immoral.

When you say "yes" and what you really wanted to say is "no," you feel guilty because you are not following your true feelings. Furthermore, you are not respecting yourself. Self-respect gives you the power to make your own choices. Other people do not decide for you. You decide for yourself. Every time you do something that conflicts with your values and core beliefs, you will most likely feel guilty.

Manipulators control you through guilt. The main objective of the manipulator is to control you. When someone manipulates you, they are violating your personal space.

The manipulator will identify a weakness in you; show you how he/she is going to help you with it, then control you with it.

Many times you allow the manipulator to control you because of your inability to say "no." The reason you do this is to not feel guilty. Learn to say "no."

When you become aware of the manipulator's world, the manipulator is powerless!

It is possible to live a life free of guilt.

It is up to you!

Chapter 9

CONNECT WITH YOUR INSTINCTS, CONNECT WITH WEALTH

Your instincts are a gift from God and wealth is everywhere for you to have as part of the Creator's gifts. The reason you may not be experiencing wealth is because of your mental process. You might have allowed the "poverty mentality" to enter your mind. However, I have good news. You can change it!

Poverty is Like a Mental Disease

Having a poverty mentality means we are not at ease with the idea of having. Poverty mentality is a distorted way of thinking about money, prosperity, and wealth. Poverty mentality can be cured by replacing it with a wealth mentality.

The best way to help poor people is to not become one of them. Stay away from people who suffer from poverty mentality. It is highly contagious!

Why do you suffer from the pain of poverty mentality? Probably because you did not know you could be helped. If you have a pain in any part of your body, you would not think twice to seek help. Why don't you do the same thing with the pain of poverty mentality?

According to the dictionary, disease means:

1. A condition of the body in which there is an incorrect function, resulting from the effect of heredity, infection, diet, or environment.
2. Any harmful or destructive condition.
3. Any abnormal condition.
4. Antidote = health, cure.

Let's analyze what the dictionary says about disease, and see how it relates to poverty mentality.

1. A Condition of the Body in Which There is an Incorrect Function Resulting From the Effect of Heredity, Infection, Diet, or Environment

Have you ever seen people who were born to wealth who never experience money problems? The reason is because of their heredity and their environment, they developed a wealth mentality from the start. If by accident, these people were to lose their money, they would get it right back.

Now, let's discuss infection and diet. Infecting our minds is what people do when they program us with "poverty mentality," and diet is what we continue to feed our minds every day.

"Lack mentality" is feeling there is not enough to go around for everyone. "Poverty mentality" is believing you do not deserve to have. Lack mentality is part of poverty mentality.

How often have you heard the following: "Money does not grow on trees!"

This type of message programs your mind with a poverty mentality.

You have the power to change your diet (the thoughts you feed your subconscious mind) and keep your mind clean from poverty thoughts. Do not allow yourself or any one else to infect your mind with poverty thinking.

2. Any Harmful or Destructive Condition

What this means is that poverty is the thinking process in your mind that is harmful and destructive. The reason some people think this way is because they were programmed in this manner.

Some religions have emphasized the poverty mentality by preaching to the masses that it is a virtue . As a matter of fact, one of the messages we may have received is that the more you suffer, the more God loves you.

How can a loving God want his children to suffer? Does this make sense to you? Not to me! God wants us to have, and to have abundantly.

Some societies have, unfortunately, allowed the continuance of the poverty mentality. This is evident in some third world countries.

3. An Abnormal Condition

Disease is an abnormal condition. Poverty mentality is an abnormal condition, and you have the power to change it.

Now, how do you change it? With the following:

4. The Antidote to Disease is Health and Cure

You have the power to cure yourself and remove the poverty mentality by controlling the diet (messages) that go into your subconscious.

Your job will be to have a conscious awareness and constantly change your negative thinking about prosperity to a positive one.

My Toilet Paper Story

I have had to fight the poverty mentality, and one funny way I discovered one of the manifestations of my poverty mentality was my toilet paper story.

I used to buy the least expensive toilet paper, and for years my husband told me I suffered from a poverty mentality. He said if I were to buy the more expensive toilet paper, I would not only have a more pleasant experience when using it, but I would save money at the same time. After years of his persisting I buy a more expensive paper, I finally purchased the better quality toilet paper, and to my surprise it lasted longer. So, I not only saved money, but also realized that indeed it was certainly an extremely pleasant experience!

Money Does not Grow on Trees

In my childhood I always heard, "Money does not grow on trees." What this expression did was further my poverty mentality because I felt there was not enough to go around.

Whenever I wanted a new toy or simply wanted something else, my family would say, "Money does not grow on trees." Consequently, this reinforced the thought that if I had a money tree in my back yard, I would never have any problems.

I realized I am my money tree! With God's help, I have been able as an adult to reverse my thinking and create a mentality that empowers me to live in abundance.

If you Suffer from of Poverty Mentality, here are Some Steps you Can Take to Help Cure Yourself:

1. Admit there is a problem.
2. Ask God to show you the mental patterns (your thoughts on poverty) that keep you away from your God-given right of experiencing wealth.
3. Start taking steps today towards changing your negative mental patterns.
4. Use the power of affirmation to change your negative patterns.
5. Work on your self-esteem. The more you feel worthy of having wealth, and believe you deserve the best in life, the more you will attract wealth.
6. Become comfortable with the idea of having money. Money is just a medium of exchange.
7. Every day do something that makes you feel worthy.
8. Count your blessings. When you have a grateful heart, blessings multiply.

I believe we were born perfect with a connection to God's wealth. God is abundance. For example, look at the ocean. Man has eaten from the ocean since the beginning of time, and there are still plenty of fish. We take extra fish and freeze them, and yet we do not deplete the ocean's supply. Neither can we deplete the ocean of water.

Open yourself to create wealth. I dedicate this chapter to you, to help you connect with your instincts and create wealth. Remember, wealth is a God-given right!

What is Wealth?

According to the dictionary, wealth is:

1. A great quantity of money or property of value.
2. A plentiful amount.
3. All goods that have a monetary or exchange value.
4. Anything that has utility and is capable o exchange.
5. The state of being rich; prosperity and affluence.
6. Happiness.

Wealth is to have all of your needs (instincts) met abundantly and balanced at a physical, emotional, and spiritual level, and still have plenty to share with others. Wealth is to be healthy and happy!

Wealth is Much More than Money

There are some who believe money is evil. Money is neither good nor bad. Money is just money. Money is a medium of exchange and a measure of value. Before money, goods and services were exchanged on a value-for-value basis. Money allows us to store its value for future use. For example, you save money today in a retirement account for a future date when you will need it.

Money allows you to save and collect the benefits of the fruits of your labor for spending at a future time. Thus, it becomes the prime factor providing future security as well as facilitating the needs of survival in present day life. Because of this, money is an integral part of such things as prosperity, riches, abundance, and happiness. It is the facilitator of all of life's material transactions.

You cannot have material riches without money. Thus, if you want riches, begin to get comfortable with the purpose and use of money.

Just having money does not make you wealthy! Contrary to popular belief, wealth is much more than that.

Wealth is a feeling that can be created. This is why when a wealthy person losses all of their possessions, they almost always recover everything because they have the feeling of wealth. This is because they feel wealthy inside. The Universe uses the law of attraction and directs the wealth back to them.

Remember, feelings are always followed by thoughts.

THE OBJECTIVE IS TO FIRST THINK WEALTHY, THEN TO FEEL WEALTHY, AND THEN TO ATTRACT WEALTH.

You Can Feel Wealthy by Knowing in Your Heart that You Can Fulfill Your Instincts. This Means Feeling Able to Satisfy:

1. The Social Instinct. To have a good relationship

with yourself and a good relationship with others. Having a good relationship with yourself includes feeling that you have good self-esteem and self-respect, you are capable of being a friend to yourself and others, to feel important, useful, valuable, respected, and that you are satisfied with your work and achievements.

2. **The Security Instinct.** To feel you are capable of having food, clothing, shelter, money, time, talent, information, opportunity, and clear boundaries of who you are physically, emotionally, and spiritually (personal space). To feel able to communicate your feelings and opinions to others, and to accept others' opinions and feelings in return.

3. **The Sexual Instincts.** To feel satisfied with your sexual identity of being masculine or feminine, paternal or maternal, attractive or attracted, and feeling satisfied with your sexual relations.

WHEN YOU CAN CONNECT WITH AND FULFILL ALL OF YOUR INSTINCTS AND SHARE THEM WITH OTHERS, YOU WILL BE WEALTHY!

Wealth is:

Health ---- Health is more than the absence of illness. Health is having vitality and energy. If you are blessed with health, give thanks to the Universe because you are wealthy. Emerson said, "Our primary wealth is our health."

Happiness --- Happiness is a feeling that things are great, right at this moment.

Prosperity --- Prosperity is to satisfy all of your needs and wants abundantly by flourishing and being successful, especially financially.

Riches ------ Riches can be in various forms. It could be money, talents, creativity, ideas, wisdom, love.

Abundance – Abundance is having your needs and wants met with more to share. It is a feeling you can give without sacrificing your needs.

Knowing what you want ---- Being in touch with your true Self and knowing what your heart desires gives you a sense of purpose.

Learning --- Learning is being open to new information God might be placing in your path. With the proper use of what we learn, we achieve wisdom.

Loving ---- Love yourself unconditionally. Once you love yourself, then you can love others. The more love you give, the more you will have to give.

Caring ---- Caring is loving with compassion. It is a real concern about the other person.

Follow Your Instincts

Enjoying --- Enjoying is experiencing the beauty in things. It is to experience pleasure with joy.

Friendship ---- Friendship is being a friend and having friends.

Sharing/Service --- Sharing is giving of yourself, giving time, energy, love, compassion, companionship, friendship, humor, talents, and ideas. Service is the vehicle to experience sharing. Service is an act of assistance.

Wealth is sharing!

If you have time	-----	Share time
If you have money	-----	Share money
If you have knowledge	-----	Share knowledge
If you have love	-----	Share love

You can always find something to share – Give and the Universe will multiply it

Balance ---------- Create balance while experiencing health, happiness, prosperity, riches, abundance, knowing what you want, learning, loving, caring, friendship, enjoying, and sharing/service. Balance is the most important of them all.

In the physical aspect, wealth is to have plenty to take care of your body in ways such as eating, exercising, getting massages, grooming your hair and nails, etc.

In the emotional, wealth is to be connected with your instincts and feelings, and to be at peace with yourself and having serenity.

In the spiritual, wealth is to be connected with the Universe via intuition and your instincts.

YOU CAN BEGIN TO FEEL WEALTHY TODAY!

Feeling Wealthy is a Feeling You Can Create Yourself

My husband and I were going to try out our new pool water heater, and I wanted to have a glass of wine to celebrate the occasion, but my husband does not drink wine. For this reason, I had been buying small bottles of wine that come 4 bottles in a little case for $3.99. However, the wine that I like is a $25.00 bottle of Pouilly-Fuisse. I opened one of the small wine bottles and after I served it, I asked myself, "What would a wealthy person do in this case?" Probably open the Pouilly-Fuisse, even if they would only have one glass, and discard the rest. I opened the Pouilly-Fuisse bottle and drank my glass of wine, and threw away the rest. When I did this, I felt very wealthy.

My question to you is: "What can you do today that will make you feel wealthy?"

Remember, feeling wealthy is just a feeling. Take small steps to begin connecting with the feeling of wealth.

Once you feel wealthy inside, and *follow your instincts*, then you will attract wealth by the law of attraction. *Start feeling wealthy today!*

Wealth and Your Self-image

Our self-image is like a barometer. It will adjust our lives to what we think we are worth. For example: If you happen

Follow Your Instincts

to be in sales and you have a limiting thought that your income can only be $1,000 a week, but one week you happen to sell $1,200, then, since your (self-image) is programmed to only make $1,000, the following week you will probably only make $800, which brings you back to your average of $1,000 a week.

Another example is that you might get a bonus, but if you do not think you deserve this bonus, your barometer will create an event to force you to use this money and not be able to enjoy it. For example, your car breaks down and the cost of repairing it is exactly the same amount as the bonus.

Sometimes it is difficult to believe our income is connected to our self-image, but it is. What this means is your self-image decides your worth and how much happiness you deserve.

You Become Part of Your Environment

Our self-image, thoughts, and feelings are constantly being shaped by our surroundings. We become part of our environment. None of us are immune to outside influences. We are very susceptible to the influences of other people around us. We have to become aware of what other people, especially our closest family members, co-workers, friends, and the media, are saying – how they are expressing themselves and how it affects us.

If our thoughts and our feelings are constantly being shaped by our surroundings, it is fair to say our environment is shaping our goals and our actions as well.

There is an expression that says, "Show me your

friends, and I will tell you who you are." I believe this to be true. Have you ever noticed that if you associate with a depressing person, before you know it, you feel depressed also, or to the contrary, if you are with a positive person, you become positive?

My Secretary Story

When I first interviewed Maria for a secretarial possition, she said she did not have much office work experience. She had worked as a cleaning lady at a hotel and as a part-time secretary in a doctor's office. However, she had the responsibility of raising two children and needed a job. Maria said, "If you give me an opportunity and train me, you will never be sorry." Her words impressed me, and I hired her at a salary of $6.50 an hour, when at the time minimum wage was $5.50.

I really liked Maria and took her under my wing, training her, and helping her to develop skills to run an office. In addition, she grew emotionally and spiritually.

In recognition of her desire to learn, I gave her a raise every time she improved in a particular area. In just one year, Maria went from making $6.50 to $9.50 an hour. Also, as a sign of my appreciation, I treated her to massages, a day in a spa, special treats to fancy restaurants, and Christmas bonuses that allowed her to go on vacations she never dreamed possible. I helped introduce Maria to a life of abundance.

Later, I hired Jennifer, who turned out to be a manipulative and negative person, and who was quite subtle in her ways.

Jennifer was either jealous of Maria or wanted her

position, and began to tell Maria she was not appreciated, and deserved a better paying job. She also began to tell her negative things about other people in the office, making Maria's time at the office very difficult. Unfortunately, Maria began to believe Jennifer.

Jennifer asked for a personal week off, and I said okay. The week Jennifer was off, Maria, without any notice to me, did not come to work. As the morning progressed and I did not hear from Maria, I became concerned something happened because this was not like her. I called her home, but there was no answer. That afternoon, Jennifer arrived and brought a three-line letter from Maria indicating that she quit. I could not believe Maria would have behaved this way.

I called her home again a few times, but to this day I have not heard from Maria.

I realized Jennifer was a negative instigator, and I had no choice, but to fire her upon her return. There is, without exception, no room in my life for negativity.

The point of this story is to show that you become part of your surroundings. Maria started listening to someone who was negatively manipulative, and she became part of that negativism that finally cost her her job. Unfortunately, Maria lost her opportunity to continue to grow financially, emotionally, and spiritually. Sadly, later on I learned Maria was making less money.

Become very aware of who you listen to and associate with because one thing is certain: you become part of your environment!

If you are serious about becoming wealthy and prosperous, get serious about the people you allow in your life.

My question to you is: What kind of person do you want to be shaping your goals and actions?

Have you noticed that when you mix with enthusiastic people, you get filled with enthusiasm? If you mix with happy people, you are happy. If you mix with prosperous people, you end up prosperous. You first have to decide what you want in life, and then, surround yourself with the people who support that decision.

IF YOU WANT WEALTH AND PROSPERITY, SURROUND YOURSELF WITH PEOPLE WHO ARE WEALTHY AND PROSPEROUS.

What Can You do Today to Improve Your Finances?

1. Recognize your poverty mentality. You can change it, if you believe you can. It is up to you!

2. Analyze your belief system, if it is stopping you from achieving your financial success. If you are unhappy with your financial position, your belief system is the problem. Work on changing your negative patterns into positive ones by using the power of affirmations.
Example: "I never earn enough money." Change this statement to: "I earn all the money I need and want."

3. Dedicate yourself to becoming prosperous. Put forth the necessary energy to achieve financial success.

4. Observe wealthy people. Surround yourself with people who have achieved the level of success you desire. Study their qualities and begin to develop those qualities yourself.

5. Be humble and ask for help from those who already have what you want.

6. Make a list of everyone you owe money to and make a plan to pay them. By acknowledging your debts, you are affirming that you will have the money to pay them. In turn, the Universe will assist you in paying your debts, and it will reward you with even more abundance.

7. Save first and spend later. Poor people spend first and save later, and stay poor.

8. Stop blaming others for your lack of prosperity. It is up to you to change your finances.

9. Set goals and have a plan to achieve them.

10. Most importantly, constantly re-affirm to yourself you deserve to be prosperous. Use the power of affirmation to accomplish this.

The path to prosperity is to satisfy your needs first and then achieve your wants.

"Act as If" You Have Already Achieved Wealth!

Have you ever heard the expression "Act as if." The more you "act as if" you are wealthy, the more you will feel wealthy, and the more you feel wealthy, the faster you will attract wealth.

While I was trying to develop my wealth mentality, I decided that I would do certain things that made me feel wealthy.

1. I hired a cleaning lady.
2. When I went grocery shopping, I would buy the expensive cheese I always wanted, that before I would not give myself permission to buy, because I did not feel I deserved it. I also started buying my favorite expensive wine.
3. Began to have massages every week.
4. Hired a personal trainer for my exercises (wealthy people had one of those).
5. I hired a limousine to take the mothers out for Mothers Day, and other special occasions.
6. Went to Las Vegas and re-committed to my relationship by getting married to my husband again at the Elvis Presley Chapel. (Rich people did that). While in Las Vegas, I went to the spa everyday, making me feel like a million bucks!!!

These are some of the things I have done to make me feel wealthy. Taking these steps I attracted even more riches to my life. You can start connecting with the feeling of wealth today, beginning with taking small steps.

In my case, the wealthier I acted, the more I would think wealthy. That is the reason I made it a point to feel wealthy every day. So can you! – *What you think is what you get!*

THINK WEALTHY -- GET WEALTHY. THINK POOR – STAY POOR. YOUR PROSPERITY, OR THE LACK OF IT, IS THE RESULT OF YOUR THINKING.

Follow Your Instincts

My Husband and I Changed Our Thinking and Became Millionaires.

When I realized my prosperity, or lack of it, was a result of my thinking and years of negative programming, I decided to buy an audio tape that promised to help me become a millionaire in three years. My husband and I began to listen to this tape day and night.

At the time we began to listen to this tape, we were involved in a business that offered the potential of becoming millionaires. After a few months of listening to the tape, our business collapsed, which was quite a surprise to us because we were somewhat successful in that business!

At first, my husband and I could not understand what went wrong. Here we were programming our minds to become millionaires and our business collapsed. After a while, I understood and explained to my husband that since we had programmed our subconscious mind to become millionaires, our subconscious was responding and destroying the vehicle that was not going to take us there

There is a universal law that says, "to build the new. you have to destroy the old." The understanding of this law gave me serenity to survive very rough and difficult times.

One morning, my husband thought of visiting an old friend and mentor. The objective of the visit was to see if we could do a joint venture, starting a similar company to the one he owned, in another town close to the one we lived in. When my husband visited his friend, to my husband's surprise, his friend was looking to retire and needed someone he could trust to sell his business to. His friend offered to sell my husband the business. On a handshake, and trusting the Universe, my husband, who had been self-employed for many years, went to work for his friend in the hope of being able to buy the business in one year.

At the time of the offer, we were really amazed at the power of the subconscious mind. We did not have any money to give as a down payment, having lost all our money in the previous venture. We bought a business with no down payment, with only a mortgage to pay his friend.

Two years from the date we began to listen to the tape, we were millionaires in assets.

I am telling you these facts so you know it is possible to change your mind and change your life. My husband and I did it, so can you!

Difference Between Needs and Wants

It is okay for you to have "wants." *Your want is the moving force that motivates you to do things.* What is not okay is for you to make your wants your needs. For example, it is okay to want a bigger house, but at a instinct level what you need is shelter. When you make a want a need, you might not be able to satisfy the want for whatever reason, and then you can become frustrated.

Your primary needs are food, clothing, and shelter. Your wants would be to have designer clothes, fancy food, and an expensive house. There is nothing wrong with wanting designer clothes. What is wrong is when you are unhappy because of not having a particular style of clothing. When you clearly identify your needs, you can see they are quite basic, and your life becomes simpler. You do not have to impress anyone.

Follow Your Instincts

I need a car as a means of transportation. I want a Mercedes Benz. I do not need it. Sometimes this simple statement can make a big difference in how a person feels. I know that some people feel worthless unless they are driving a fancy car. *It is important to know the difference between needs and wants!*

I love to drive fancy cars and my husband and I love to name them. When our business first became successful, we purchased a Volvo, and we named it Eddy Volvo. Business got better, and we moved up to Larry Lexus. As business got even better, we purchased Jerry Jaguar.

Then, as I mentioned before, our business collapsed, and I had to give up Jerry Jaguar and bought Charley Chevy. The important thing to know is that I felt just as good driving my 14-year-old Chevy van as I did driving my new fancy cars. The reason was my self-esteem was not dependent on what I was driving. I am valuable no matter what car I am driving. As a matter of fact, when my husband and I went to fancy restaurants, and arrived in Charley Chevy, the parking attendants looked at us funny. We did not care. We had the money to eat at the restaurant and give them a good tip, perhaps an even better one than the people with the fancy cars.

My husband and I felt very wealthy as we drove around in Charley Chevy. We knew that feeling wealthy was totally up to us, and we were not going to allow other people's thoughts to cause us to feel any different.

Prosperity is Achieving Our Wants After We Have Taken Care of Our Needs

I believe some wants come out of needs. God places the

desire for wants inside of man as a means of helping to make progress in his life. A good example would be the washing machine. Before the washing machine, man washed clothes by hand and it took a long time. Out of the desire to be more efficient, man created a machine to perform this task. Later, out of the desire to save time drying the clothes and not have to be bound by weather conditions, he developed the dryer.

I could come up with thousands of examples of wants that arose from man's needs. The next time you have a want ask yourself, "What need am I trying to excessively satisfy."

A "want" is usually a desire to satisfy a "need" to excess. Wants are healthy, and without them there would be little progress.

Once you understand your instincts (needs), what you want to do is connect with them via intuition. The way you connect to intuition is by following your instincts all the time, even when your intellect is telling you to do something different. When you want to *follow your instincts* and your intellect is telling you to act differently, meditation can be a very helpful tool in separating your intellectual desires from your true understanding of your inner feelings (instincts). Go back to chapter one and review how to connect with and follow your intuition.

When you can meditate and discern the truth about your feelings, then you can *follow your instincts*.

Happiness is an Inside Job!

Happiness is looking at whatever happens as just part of life. When something negative happens, in order not be unhappy or sad, there has to be an acceptance that everything happens for a reason. There is no need for unhappiness because the negative can be turned into an opportunity to learn and grow.

Happiness is self-bestowed. It is up to you to be happy. A feeling starts with a thought. So, if you are unhappy, stop and ask yourself, "What was I thinking that caused this feeling?" Then, change your thinking and you will change your feeling!

If you do something you do not really want to do, you will create unhappiness in your life. Learn to say "no." Being assertive is part of loving yourself. Remember, *Happiness is an Inside Job!*

THE BOTTOM LINE REASON FOR NOT FEELING WEALTHY IS NOT FEELING WORTHY. LOW SELF-ESTEEM IS THE CAUSE OF MOST UNHAPPINESS IN THE WORLD, INCLUDING YOURS.

Here is a good affirmation for you:

I AM WORTHY OF HAVING WEALTH!

Receiving - Part of Wealth

Wealth is a feeling of being capable of receiving. For some people, receiving is difficult. It is difficult because they do not feel worthy of receiving due to low self-esteem, and/or they are not humble enough to just accept a gift.

When you allow someone else to give you something, you are giving the other person the opportunity of satisfying his or her instincts. This has been an area of my life I have had to work on a lot, and I am still doing so. It is easy for me to give, but very difficult for me to receive. The reason for my behavior is that I still need to become more humble.

If you want abundance in all areas of your life, find an area where you might have plenty, then go and share it. The Universe will compensate you in other areas.

Giving, as a Form of Service

One day, I came to realize that every time I gave a free seminar on the 12-step program (the purpose of which was to help others recover from addiction), I would prosper in some other area of my life. I started to pay attention to this miracle. The more you have and share with others, the more you will receive. Whatever you give freely, will be multiplied. Since I had plenty to give, and I gave it freely in my seminars, the Universe compensated me by creating more abundance in other areas of my life.

As you give to the Universe, so the Universe will give to you. Practice this principal and miracles will happen!

The Wealth of Friendship

I have a neighbor (Juan) who really personifies the word *service*. He claims, because he is retired, he has more time available than we do. As a matter of fact, since we moved into our house and became the best of friends, we have yet to take the garbage out. He is always ready to help in a neighborly way. Every one in the neighborhood loves Juan, especially us.

Juan says that when we allow him to help us, we are giving him the opportunity to feel valuable, useful, respected, important, appreciated, and contributing. In actuality, what he is doing is satisfying his social instinct at the personal relationship level. He's a great guy!

Next time someone is offering to help you (without any strings attached), give him or her the opportunity to help you, because by doing so, you are assisting him or her in satisfying their social instinct.

Service is giving with absolutely no desire of receiving anything in return. The compensation the Universe will bestow upon you is a fulfilled life with abundantly satisfied instincts.

The biggest service you can offer the world is to take care of yourself no matter what. When you take care of yourself and you love yourself, you are giving service to the world, because as you love yourself you will then be able to love others.

Summary

The poverty mentality means we are not at ease with the idea of having.

Poverty mentality can be cured by replacing it with a wealth mentality. If you are serious about becoming wealthy, get serious about the people you allow in your life. The best way to help poor people is to not become one of them.

What you think is what you get.
> Think poor — Stay poor.
> Think wealthy — Get wealthy.

Your wealth, or the lack of it, is the result of your thinking. Change your thinking and you will change your feelings. Feeling wealthy is a feeling you can create yourself by learning to connect with and *follow your instincts*.

The objective is to first think wealthy, then to feel wealthy, and then attract wealth!

Wealth is having health, happiness, prosperity, riches, abundance, knowing what you want, learning, loving, caring, friendship, enjoying, sharing/service and balance.

> Wealth is an Inside Job!

> And you have it!

"Wealth is the product of man's capacity to think."

- Ayn Rand

Chapter 10

FOLLOW YOUR INSTINCTS TO ACHIEVE SUCCESS, WEALTH, AND HAPPINESS

To achieve success, wealth, and happiness, the first thing you must do is work on you. *Success, Wealth, and Happiness is an Inside Job!*

Following your instincts will make you:

1. Successful

2. Wealthy

3. Happy

The goal here is to enhance the quality of your life. *Following your instincts* will assure that you will reach that goal. There is, as you know, no free lunch! Never, in my lifetime, have I acquired anything of value without putting forth the effort required. This also applies to you. It is time to start the work.

Start by Working on You

In whatever area of your life you want to be successful, the first thing you must do is to work on you. The secret of success is to believe in yourself.

You were born with the instinct blueprint as a gift from the Creator to assist you in living a productive, successful, and happy life.

When you are able to express and radiate the real you, you become the source of your abundance. Practice self-love, self-worth, self-respect, inner peace, joy, and happiness.

The greatest gift you can give yourself is the gift of knowing yourself!

When you understand, connect with, and *follow your instincts*, you can think, feel, and express exactly what you want. This allows you to control your life and create the life you want for yourself.

To accomplish great things, you must first dream, plan, and set goals, take action and finally, believe in yourself, that you can do it. Above all, believe you deserve great things to happen to you.

The primary source of success is self-esteem. It is appreciating your own worth and importance. It is what you think and feel about yourself. It is not what someone else thinks or feels about you. Finally, it is the judgment you pass on yourself. *Learn to forgive yourself for your mistakes to improve your self-esteem.*

If you see yourself thinking negatively all the time, work on your self-esteem. One of the symptoms of low self-esteem is negativity. A healthy self-esteem enables you to accept challenges, learn new things, and take risks. Remember, self-esteem is how you feel about yourself. To be successful you must have good thoughts about yourself. There is no room for negativity! Yes, you can build your self-esteem.

Your Focus Determines Your Reality

If who you are today is not working for you, change it! You can become the right person for you.

Everything you believe in was given to you. There is a big difference between what you know and what you believe. *You know by learning, you believe by experiencing.*

Thoughts, Feelings and Actions

Through working with your thoughts, feelings, and actions, you can create anything you want.

Your thoughts make up your world, and they can be changed. You can change how you see your world by the thoughts you embrace. When you are able to change a negative thought into a positive one, you are changing the outcome of your life.

You have to assume the responsibility that you create your reality. Assume the responsibility of your thoughts, feelings, and actions, and your life will take on a new meaning.

Your Thoughts Create Your Reality

Your thoughts are the cause of your reality and what happens is the effect of your thoughts. Thoughts mixed with positive feelings will become a magnetic force to attract other positive thoughts, thus creating a spiritual energy to accomplish your goals.

Sometimes you might believe the past will continue to repeat itself in the future, without the possibility of it being different. This is not so. The past does not have to be your future. When analyzing this scenario, ask yourself: "What was my thought process when I created the past reality?" Then, you can change the thought that created the past reality and create a different reality NOW. Sometimes it is difficult to change our realities when facing guilt.

Guilt is past — Fear is future — Stay in the NOW to achieve success.

You Are What You Believe

Your belief system is based on your past experience. If you are not careful, you can find yourself reliving your past. If you anticipate the future to be like the past, you create fear of the future. By examining your belief system and creating a new one, you can take charge of your life, and allow your true self to surface.

What your mind embraces becomes your life. If your belief system is one of love and peace, this is what you are going to experience. On the other hand, if your mind is filled with fear and guilt, then that is what you will encounter.

At the beginning of each day ask yourself, "Do I want to experience peace or conflict?"

The choice is yours! Which one will you choose?

The success, happiness, and inner peace you have today is related to your belief system.

Your mind is the director, producer, scriptwriter, audience and most importantly, the critic. You have the capacity to change your mind and the thoughts you embrace.

You are the director of your thoughts and your thoughts direct your life!

Your Dreams are Related to Your Belief System

The reason a lot of us do not dream big is that we do not feel worthy. The more worthy you feel, the more the Universe will give you what you want and desire.

The way to achieve dreams is to turn desire into action. Imagine you are dreaming of having a new car. Turn your dream into a desire for a new car by believing you deserve it. Once you are able to match your belief with your desire (wants), you will then take the proper steps that will lead you to owning a new vehicle and achieving your dream.

Now, suppose you want an expensive car, and you do not believe you deserve it. Because your belief system is not matching your desire (wants), you probably will not take the proper action towards achieving your dream.

Everything you have, or do not have, is related to your belief system and the big barometer is your self-esteem.

The more you believe you are worthy of having your desires and dreams come true, the easier it will be to attract them. Wanting something is not enough, having the belief you deserve it is what will attract it to your life.

Success Starts in Your Mind

Success, wealth and happiness begin in your head. You control how much or how little you achieve in these three areas.

Remember, you think first, then get a feeling, then behave in accordance with that feeling.

You must first think successful, then feel successful, which is what will lead you to the correct action or behavior to make you successful.

Achieve Success by Following Your Instincts

Success is an inside Job! If you do not believe in yourself and in what you can accomplish, nothing matters because you are not going to be successful. Success is about honoring your feelings.

Your instincts are inside you — Success is also inside you!

I believe you have the potential to become anything you want to be. Understanding, connecting with, and following your instincts will take you wherever you want to go.

Following your instincts can be one of the scariest steps you will ever take. Like anything in life, the more you do it, the easier it will become. Before you can *follow your instincts*, you have to understand them. Your instincts' purpose is to assist you in achieving success, wealth, and happiness.

When faced with direction from your inner guidance, it is necessary to make a commitment to follow that guidance, even when the direction to take is not immediately apparent.

Learn to accept direction from you inner intuitive voice. Follow your intuition or instinct. When your inner guidance gives you a direction to take, it will also provide the means for you to accomplish your goal. Your job is just to follow it!

Use your instincts to become successful concerning these areas:

1. Social
2. Security
3. Sex

1. Social

In the social area, you can achieve successful relationships with yourself and others. The success you have today is directly related to your belief system.

2. Security

In the security area, you can achieve an ongoing feeling of well being. This will encompass self-preservation and all that it represents, including food, shelter, clothing, and money as a medium of exchange. The ability to communicate your needs and wants is of prime importance concerning your security. Without it, you will not be able to enlist the assistance of others when needed.

3. Sex

In the sexual area, you can achieve a sense of wholeness, as your sexual identity is a sense of Self. The ultimate sharing of your being is when you join spiritually, emotionally, and physically with your partner.

Burning Desire is One of the Key Ingredients for Success

Just wishing for something will not bring success. You have to have a burning desire.

The next time you want something, start by creating a burning desire to have it. Then, follow it by having a definite plan of how you will get it and finally persist until you reach what you desire. There must be no room for failure.

Formula to achieve your dreams:

1. Turn a dream into a burning desire.

2. Add a definite plan of action (goal setting).

3. Follow your plan with persistence and do not allow room for failure. Your realized dreams will be the results!

In this formula to achieve your dreams, every time you encounter a failure, turn the failure in the direction of achieving your goal. Remember, failure is part of success. A small failure might just mean you need to change direction. Failure is temporary defeat, or an indication something might be wrong with your plan.

When you want something, it starts with a thought. Then, you have to add the ingredient of faith. Faith is unquestioning belief without requiring proof. When you combine thoughts with faith, you will create an energy, which will attract all the necessary ingredients and circumstances to help you achieve your dreams.

Whenever you have doubts or are afraid you will not achieve your dreams, add the ingredient of faith. *Believe it is possible!*

If you suffer from poverty mentality, you may feel doomed to failure, and these thoughts may paralyze you even before you start. To combat the poverty mentality, use the power of affirmations to create faith that it is possible.

Faith is a state of mind − You can create faith by the power of self-suggestion.

The most important faith you must develop is faith in yourself. Once you believe you can do it, you will be able to make it happen.

Faith is the force that will bring you success and is the antidote for failure. You can create the feeling of faith by the instructions you give your subconscious mind with the power of affirmations.

Follow Your Instincts

Using the Power of Affirmations to Achieve Your Success

Writing this book has been one way in which I was able to conquer my own belief system. When it was suggested I write this book, I did not believe I could do it. I was confident I had the knowledge, since I have been doing seminars on the subject for twenty years. However, I did not believe I could transform my knowledge into a book.

I made the decision to do it. The first thing I did was fight my own negative thinking. The way I accomplished this, was to order some audiotapes on becoming a writer (affirmations directing my mind that I was already a writer). I listened to these tapes for two months. I used this time to organize my thoughts on how I was going to put this information together in book form, organized my office, did market research on the subject, and finally, bought a computer to begin my project.

I started on a part-time basis, since I also helped my husband in his business, and in one year, I finished the book. Also, during this period my husband had a bad accident. He fell from a ladder and broke his leg. He was bedridden for four months. During this period, I was taking care of him and his business, and had very little time for my book.

The reason I tell you my story is two-fold. First, to show you it is possible to do anything you set your mind to. Even if you think you cannot do it, you can program your mind with affirmations. Second, if you cannot do something all at once, you can do it a little bit at a time until the task is completed.

Power of Visualization

About ten years ago, when I was living in a condominium, I decided I wanted a house. First, I wrote what kind of house I wanted and in what part of town. I wanted a three bedroom, three baths, with a big patio area for barbecues, because I love them. To assist my visualization, I went to see houses in the neighborhood I liked, and. I picked out a house.

Every day I would walk past the house and say to myself, "I own a three- bedroom, three-bath house, with a big patio area for barbecues." I would visualize I already owned a house just like that one.

Within a year, I had the money for the down payment and began shopping for my new home. The realtor showed me the very same property I had been visualizing, which was a surprise to me. The interesting part of this story is that I no longer was attracted to this particular house.

I finally purchased a four bedroom, four baths home with a large pool as a bonus, and with a wonderful barbecue area. Many times what happens, just as it did in my case, the Universe will give you more than what you visualize.

Preparation is the Key to Success

When you are undertaking a new task, it is best to plan how you will achieve it. Then, take small steps toward reaching your goal. If you make some mistakes along the way, please understand you are not a failure, and you have not failed. What is important is that you keep your eyes on the goal and celebrate your small successes.

The more successes you can put together, the more successful you will feel. Consequently, you will attract more success. It is like the "snowball effect."

It is important to notice that the preparation should be physical, emotional, and spiritual. For example:

The physical -- If you are trying to lose weight, first you need to work on the physical, which includes the food program you are going to follow. It should not be a diet, since what we are trying to accomplish is a lifelong change.

The emotional -- First, you have to work on those thought patterns that keep you away from reaching your goal. Secondly, you have to embrace thoughts that will lead you to success. In these areas you might want to find a support group.

The spiritual -- You have to ask your concept of God for the strength to persevere.

Success is Not About What Happens to You, but About How You Handle that Which Happens to You

Some people relate success only to money, but success is much more than money. You can be a success at:

1. Being a good mother/father.
2. Being a good teacher.
3. Being a good coach.
4. Being a good employer/employee.
5. Being the best you can be at whatever your goal is.

Follow Your Instincts to Achieve Success, Wealth, & Happiness

Success is inside you, waiting to come out. It is up to you to manifest it. To be successful, the first thing you must do is master yourself! Self-knowledge is the key to success.

Do a personal inventory to find out what negative traits are keeping you away from your goal!

By knowing, understanding, connecting with, and following your instincts, you will have the tools to become as successful as you want to become.

Follow Your Instincts and Say "No"

Sometimes passing on what seems to be a good opportunity is the right thing to do. I clearly remember the day I presented Jim with a real estate venture that to me was a winner. Twenty-five years ago, I was not that connected with my instincts to know any different.

After presenting Jim with the project, I remember him saying to me, "Lillian, this deal seems right. All the numbers look right. It has the right people involved in the deal. However, my gut feeling is to say 'no'." He went on to explain, "You see, what I do is analyze a project and if everything seems right, but at a gut level it does not feel right, I pass. All my life I have done this and the few times I have not followed this feeling, it hit me right in the face. It has nothing to do with you. I hope you understand, and hope my decision will not affect our relationship, but I am going to say no."

I could not understand what my friend was doing, and how he could pass on such a great opportunity. I respected his decision and assured him that our relationship would not be affected. I proceeded with the other group.

Follow Your Instincts

A year later some things happened and the deal collapsed. A few months later, I met Jim, and he reminded me of his feelings, saying one more time, "I always follow my instincts." This experience was my first exposure to wanting to understand, connect with, and follow my instincts. I learned a valuable lesson: always follow my gut feelings, my instincts!

The key is to *follow your instincts* and be willing to have the courage to say "no".

When it is imperative you say "no" because saying "no" will allow you to keep focused on your goals and enhance the chance of success, you must do so. If not, you will pay the price.

Often, it will require you to absolutely, with firmness, stick to your decision and say "no". The benefit of your assertiveness will be increased enthusiasm and energy available to accomplish your goal.

Think Big

Since your thoughts create your reality, why not think big! You can create an even better reality for yourself, when you learn to think in bigger and better ways.

Every time you think of a goal or something you want, begin to practice seeing yourself achieving even bigger and better things than what you originally thought. Practice thinking big, and you will begin to see miracles occur.

The path to thinking big is your imagination. Use your imagination to daydream and fantasize. You have to embrace an attitude that everything you imagine is possible. Whenever you see yourself saying or thinking things like, "That is impossible; it is too much money; I cannot achieve that, etc.", it is necessary to change these thoughts. Use the power of affirmations.

Dare to think Big!

As you expand your thinking and begin to think big, your ability to manifest your dream will develop. You cannot create something if you do not believe you can have it. Live your dreams in your mind first, and think big, and the equivalent reality will manifest itself.

First create what you want in a thought, and then take the necessary steps to achieve it, followed by the right positive emotion to accelerate the manifestation.

Think big and you will attract big results.

It is Never Too Late to Think Big

Sometimes you might feel it is too late to start a new venture. No matter what your age, it is never too late. For Example:

1. Ray Kroc started "McDonalds" at age 52.

2 Colonel Saunders started "Kentucky Fried Chicken" at age 65.

If you do not do it now, someone else will. Have you ever seen someone else accomplish your dream?

THE TIME TO ACHIEVE YOUR DREAM IS NOW!

Follow Your Instincts

Act Versus React

Some people live their lives being in control. They act rather than react. Others, on the other hand, do not act, but rather react. The people that act guide the course of events that surround them, whereas the people who react are subject to chance, many times reacting out of necessity to things they do not control. Their lives are usually in crisis.

What you want to do is act, not react!

When making a decision there are only two choices:

1. Doing nothing, when it is the right thing to do, puts you in control. If you do nothing when something should be done, you leave yourself open to chance. Life controls you.

2. Do something. Take charge. Control your life.

If you are one who acts, you will usually find yourself in control of your life and treating your existence from what might be considered a management position. If you are one who reacts, you will usually find yourself living a life of confusion and crisis.

Your life today is the result of the choices you've made!

You will find that when you act, rather than react, you will be practicing an essential part of the success formula.

Achieve Wealth by Following Your Instincts.

Wealth is to have all your needs (instincts) met abundantly and balanced at a physical, emotional, and spiritual level, and still have plenty to share with others. Wealth is to be healthy and happy!

Wealth is a reasonable balance between all those factors that make our lives worth living. Such wonderful and joyous things as health, happiness, prosperity, riches, abundance, knowing what you want, learning, loving, caring, friendship, enjoying and sharing enhance our lives beyond our fondest dreams. All this can be attained in the most natural way – simply by following your instincts.

Wealth is not only having money, it is much more! Wealth is a feeling that can be achieved. To have wealth you have to match your efforts with your belief system.

Whatever you have in your life right now is directly related to how worthy you feel. In order to have more wealth, you have to increase your worthiness. You can transcend the place that holds you. This can be accomplished through the power of affirmations.

Create Money by Following Your Instincts.

Money is not just for special people who have a talent or a special skill. Money is abundant for all those who claim it. You have inside you a resource to attract money to yourself. Once you have decided on a particular amount, all you need to do is ask the Universe how to get it and then *follow your instincts* to achieve it.

Creating money is the result of thinking, feeling, and acting in the direction that will help you to achieve it. Once you are clear about where you are going, then ask God for directions and *follow your instincts*. You will receive the money you desire.

Money is energy. To attract money, all you have to do is think abundantl, and then, follow your instincts to honor yourself and honor your self-worth. With the power of your thinking you can learn to master money, instead of money mastering you. When you feel worthy of having money, you will attract the right people and events at exactly the right time.

One of the fastest ways to acquire money is helping others to achieve their goals. Since money is energy, when you combine forces with others of similar thinking, the synergistic effect is unsurpassed. We often find our goals and the goals of those we assist are interconnected.

There are Two Ways to Create Money

1. The spiritual path to money.

This means you should connect to the essence inside you that can help you create the feeling of having money. Hence, you will attract it to your life through the law of attraction. When using this law, you will attract money that only serves for your highest good.

2. The man-made path to money.

This path includes: planning what you want, goal setting, time management, marketing and business planning.

You can create money by using either path, but for best results it is a good idea to keep them in balance.

Form follows thought. By having new thoughts about money, you can create new ways of acquiring it. Your thoughts are a powerful broadcasting station.

If you send out positive ideas about money that is what you will receive. The reverse is also true. If you send out negative ideas about money, you will experience a negative result. Your thoughts create your reality about money and everything else in your life.

You must embrace your capacity to create money. You are the source of your abundance. Work on your thought, feeling, and action process, and you will be surprised at the changes you will create. Mastering the process of utilizing your thoughts, feelings, and actions will lead you to acquire money.

Your thinking, combined with your feelings, followed by the appropriate action is your path to create anything you want.

Begin to think about what you want, instead of what you do not want. Positive thoughts about what you want will draw those things to you. Negative thoughts, such as fear, will draw the realization of that fear. Control your thoughts, and you will control the results.

It is important you not feel bad about having negative thoughts. Simply say, "cancel, cancel" and change the thought to a positive one.

Follow Your Instincts

Example: "I do not have enough money." Just say, "Cancel, cancel, I have an abundance of money." This new thought will draw the money to you.

Positive thoughts are far more powerful than negative thoughts. One positive thought can cancel out hundreds of negative ones.
There is great power in repeating positive thoughts. Doing so, you will accelerate creating your reality. Affirmations are positive thoughts that are repeated over and over. Affirm what you want in the present, as if you already have it.

Achieve Happiness by Following Your Instincts.

Can you just decide to be happy?

ABSOLUTELY!

You control your thoughts. You can make the decision to be happy.
Happiness is a matter of choice. Again, Abraham Lincoln said, "Most folks are as happy as they make up their minds to be." *Happiness is an Inside Job!*
Happiness is self-bestowed. It is up to you to be happy. A feeling starts with a thought. So, if you are unhappy, STOP and ask yourself, "What was I thinking that caused this feeling?" Then, change your thinking, and you will change your feeling!
Happiness is looking at whatever happens simply as part of life. When something negative happens, in order not be

to be unhappy or sad, there has to be an acceptance that everything happens for a reason. There is no need for unhappiness because the negative can be turned into an opportunity to learn and grow.

Share happiness. If you see someone without a smile, give them one of yours!

Peace of Mind as the Path to Happiness

To achieve happiness you should connect with your sense of worthiness. Feeling unworthy of enjoyment can destroy your path to happiness. Happiness is having the capacity to enjoy.

There are two primary barriers to happiness: unworthiness and ungratefulness.

Unworthiness tells you that you are not good enough to have what you want. Furthermore, unworthiness tells you that you are not good enough for what you already have. This is the primary reason why some people who have achieved certain success sabotage themselves into losing it. Feeling unworthy is the primary cause for an unhappy life.

Ungratefulness is the other side of the coin. It takes the position that what you have is not good enough for you. This is an automatic way to close the door to abundance.

Unworthiness and ungratefulness destroy your capacity to enjoy.

If you want happiness, start by working on your self-esteem to increase your sense of worthiness and begin to practice gratitude. Become grateful for even the smallest things in your life.

Follow Your Instincts

Peace of Mind as Your Single Goal

Make peace of mind the most important goal in your life every single day, and your life will take on a new meaning. For example, if you are afraid of what might happen tomorrow, say to yourself: "Today all I have to do is stay in the present."
How many times do you worry about something that never occurs? Let the future be the future!

Peace of mind is achieved by embracing positive thoughts and staying in the present moment.

Count Your Blessings

The fastest way to a happy life is a grateful heart. Sometimes it is difficult to become happy when we are in a negative frame of mind. The way to come out of this state of mind is to become grateful.
Think back to your basic needs. The Universe has always provided air, food, water, clothing, and shelter. Also, if you really analyze your life, all of your instincts have been satisfied throughout. These are blessings. Furthermore, if you really look closely, a number of wants have also been satisfied along the way. Look at your life and see how many gifts you have beyond your basic needs.
So, make a list today of all the gifts from the Universe, and you will automatically be happier.
Sometimes we can become so involved in our wants that we forget to enjoy what we have now. Do not make this mistake. While it is nice to think about and want better things, it is important to enjoy what we have right now. This attitude opens doors for more.

The Present is a Gift

Usually we are either in the past or in the future, but the objective of happiness is to be in the present, in the now. A lot of us spend too much time in the future or in what has already happened to us. While it is important to study our past to learn from our mistakes, it does not mean we have to stay there. *Stay in the Now!*

Living in the Present -- My Nephew's Story that Changed My Thinking

I remember one day driving on the expressway with my five-year-old nephew sitting in the passenger seat. Normally, when we were in the car together, we would talk. That day, I was in one of my "poor me" moods, and my nephew said to me, "Auntie, look at the moon, it's red!" This woke me up, and I realized he was missing my presence and with childhood wisdom, he was saying, "get out of that negative space and be here with me."

When I realized what I was doing, I thanked him for showing me the moon, and began to carry on a conversation like always. He helped me get out of my own thinking and share with him. Children can be great teachers, if we let them.

Staying in the now is achieved by constantly controlling your thinking. When you see yourself thinking either of the past or the future, just direct your thinking to the now. It is challenging, but it can be done!

Once you achieve being in the now, you have to become aware of whether you are focusing your thinking negatively or positively. Each moment contains good and bad, positive and negative. It is up to you to focus on the positive! This practice will lead you to happiness!

Good or Bad Luck is Created by Your Own Thinking

Did you ever believe your happiness was determined by your environment, the events in your life, the reactions other people had toward you, or that your happiness was determined by your good or bad luck?

This thinking is a great way to avoid responsibility. Your own thinking creates good or bad luck, you just have to assume the responsibility for your happiness. *Happiness is an inside job!* You are responsible for your thoughts, and in essence, for the reality you create.

A good affirmation is:

I am responsible for my thoughts and what I create.

Each day is an opportunity to choose what you think, and in doing so, you create your reality.

Open the Doors to Success, Wealth, and Happiness by Making a Gratitude List.

One of the fastest ways to open yourself to success, wealth, and happiness is having a grateful heart. I remember a period of my life in which I almost died of anorexia. I was very depressed and unhappy. A spiritual healer suggested I make a list of 50 things I was grateful for. I was in such a negative space that when I called her, I only had five items on my list. She said, "My dear, that is just not good enough, the list has to be 50 items or more with no excuses. Think of the little things in your life that are gifts from the Creator, such as the fact that you can see, walk, talk, etc. Many times we take these gifts for granted. Call me tomorrow and this list better be more than 50 items."

That night I began to see life differently. My whole life took on a new meaning, and I began to come out of my depression and travel the road to happiness. I truly believe this simple assignment saved my life.

Now, when I get up in the morning, the first thing I do is be grateful and give thanks for the new day, a new beginning. What a gift to be here one more day! Then, I give thanks to my Creator for all of the other gifts he bestowed upon my family and me.

My assignment to you is:

Make a list of 50 items or more that you are grateful for.

I hope this tool will bring you as much joy and happiness as it has brought me.

SUMMARY

You were born with the instinct blueprint as a gift from the Creator to assist you to live a successful, wealthy, and happy life.

To accomplish great things, you must first dream, plan, and set goals, then act. Finally, you must believe in yourself, that you can do it, and that you deserve good things to happen to you.

Your thoughts create your reality. Why not think big! As you expand your thinking and begin to think big, your ability to manifest your dream will develop. Live your dreams in your mind first, think big, and the equivalent reality will manifest itself.

Create what you want first in a thought, then take the necessary steps to achieve it, and *follow your instincts* to success.

Wealth is to have all of your needs met abundantly and balanced at a physical, emotional, and spiritual level, and still have plenty to share with others. Wealth is to be healthy and happy!

Whatever you have in your life right now is directly related to how worthy you feel. In order for you to have more wealth, you have to increase your worthiness. You can transcend the place that holds you. This can be accomplished through the power of affirmations.

Creating money is the result of thinking, feeling, and acting in the direction that will help you achieve it. Once you are clear about where you are going, ask God for directions and *follow your instincts.*

Happiness is a matter of choice. It is self-bestowed. The fastest way to a happy life is a grateful heart – count your blessings!

Follow Your Instincts to Achieve Success, Wealth, & Happiness

You have a sixth sense inside you. All you have to do is *follow your instincts* to success, wealth, and happiness.

EMBRACE LIFE AND KNOW YOU ARE THE BEST GIFT THE CREATOR GAVE YOU!

Good Luck!

**Congratulate yourself
for
following your instincts in purchasing
this book**

I would love to hear from you in how
this book transformed your life.

E-mail your messages to:
www.followyourinstincts.net

Monterrey Publishing, Inc.
15476 N. W. 77 Court # 706
Miami Lakes, Florida 33016

1-800 731-8887
Miami 1-305-558-1977

Visit our Web site at: www.followyourinstincts.net